PANTHER

PANTHER

A PICTORIAL HISTORY OF THE BLACK PANTHERS AND THE STORY BEHIND THE FILM

MARIO VAN PEEBLES

**ULA Y. TAYLOR
AND J. TARIKA LEWIS**

PROLOGUE BY MELVIN VAN PEEBLES

A NEWMARKET PICTORIAL MOVIEBOOK
NEWMARKET PRESS • NEW YORK

95   96   97   98   10   9   8   7   6   5   4   3   2   1

Library of Congress Cataloging-in-Publication Data
Van Peebles, Mario.
Taylor, Ula Y..
Lewis, J. Tarika.

Panther: the pictorial history of the black panthers and the story behind the film /
historical text by Ula Y. Taylor & J. Tarika Lewis:
prologue by Melvin Van Peebles: movie text by Mario Van Peebles
                    p. cm. — (A Newmarket pictorial moviebook)
ISBN 1-55704-233-0 — 1-55704-227-6 (ppk.)
1. Panther (Motion picture)—literature. 2. Black Panther Party—literature.
3. Black power—United States—History—literature. 4. United States—Race relations—literature. I. Lewis,
J. Tarika II. Title III. Series.
E185.615.T397 1995
327.73—dc20
95-7689   CIP

Quantity Purchases
Companies, professional groups, clubs, and other organizations may qualify for special terms when ordering quantities of this title. For information, write: Special Sales Department, Newmarket Press, 18 East 48th Street, New York, NY
10017. Phone: (212) 832-3575; Fax: (212) 832-3629.

Produced by Newmarket Productions, a division of Newmarket Publishing & Communications Corporation:
Esther Margolis, director; Keith Hollaman, editor; Joe Gannon, production manager; Ruth Mannes, assistant editor.

Project Editor: Jean Highland
Book design: Tania Garcia
Manufactured in the United States of America

Other Newmarket Pictorial Moviebooks include:
The Age of Innocence: A Portrait of the Film based on the Novel by Edith Wharton
Bram Stoker's Dracula: The Film and the Legend
Dances with Wolves: The Illustrated Story of the Epic Film
Far and Away: The Illustrated Story of a Journey from Ireland to America in the 1890s
Gandhi: A Pictorial Biography
The Inner Circle: An Inside View of Soviet Life Under Stalin
Last Action Hero: The Official Moviebook
Neil Simon's Lost in Yonkers: The Illustrated Screenplay of the Film
Rapa Nui: The Easter Island Legend on Film
Wyatt Earp: The Film and the Filmmakers
Wyatt Earp's West: Images and Words
Mary Shelley's Frankenstein: The Classic Tale of Terror Reborn on Film

"A people who have suffered so much for so long at the hands of a racist society must draw the line somewhere."

—from Executive Mandate No.1, the statement prepared by Huey P. Newton, Minister of Defense, and delivered by Bobby Seale, Chairman of the Black Panther Party for Self-Defense, May 2, 1967, at the state capitol in Sacramento, California.

Special Thanks

The authors and publisher wish to thank the following for their special contributions to this book:

Mario Van Peebles: I'd like to acknowledge my mother for showing me the mountain, my father for teaching me how to climb it, and the founders of the Black Power Movement who understood that a people who do not know their history are doomed to repeat it.

Thanks to my co-authors Ula Taylor and Tarika Lewis, our designer Tania Garcia, our editor the industrious Jean Highland, the resourceful assistant editor Ruth Mannes, boss lady Esther Margolis, hard-working Adam Powers, Emory Douglas for his illustrations, Sam Brooks for his original newspapers, Linda Madden, the fax woman, David Hilliard and Elaine Brown for their support, Momma Shelley Bonus, Jonathan Eubanks, Roz Payne, Howard Bingham, Ron Riesterer at The Oakland Tribune, Ward Sharrer from the Sacramento Bee, Robert Zuckerman, the punctual Graham Stumpf, Petey ("D'ho"), Preston "Shaft" Holmes, the lean and mean Dick Gregory, "Big Cheese" Michael Kuhn, Peter Graves, Joanne Muellman, foxy Adriene Bowles, Claudia Gray, Hardwood, Rick Finkelstein, David Daugherty and Steven Flynn for their support of this project from the very beginning, Tobie and Dennis Haggerty, Paul "the Roach Man", Brother "B", Maria, Pizza, Free, my critical redhead sister, and last but not least, Oscar Michaux, for the inspiration.

Ula Taylor: It's been an honor to work with J. Tarika Lewis on this book. Our text is a result of her diligent work ethic and sincere commitment to preserve the history of the Black Panther Party. I greatly appreciate the kindness of Mr. Sam Brooks. Mr. Brooks allowed me to spend countless days in his home combing through his legendary Black Panther Party archive. Discussions with Rori and Gloria Abernethy assisted in my understanding of the Party, and I appreciate their support. Ruth Mannes of Newmarket Press worked far beyond the call of duty, for which I am thankful. As always, my dear friend Otis Campbell has been supportive and patient during the course of this project.

J. Tarika Lewis: I want to acknowledge the creator, African ancestors, and those freedom fighters who lost their lives during the struggle. To the memory of my father, John Henry Lewis and my mother, Mrs. Lewis. My children and grandchildren. And for the support and encouragement from Kathleen Cleaver, Bobby Seale, Eldridge Cleaver, Emory Douglas, David Hilliard, Rori and Gloria Abernethy, Sam Brooks, Kentake Neal, and Paul Alkebulan. I also appreciate the efforts of all involved in the making of the movie. And a special thank you to the ancestors for bringing Ula Taylor and me together.

The publisher wishes to acknowledge Polygram Filmed Entertainment and Gramercy Pictures and thank them for their assistance and support with this book project; also, those who especially helped to make this book idea a reality—the talented, patient designer, Tania Garcia; our tireless, skillful editorial group, Keith Hollaman, Jean Highland, Ruth Mannes, Erika Goldman, Norman Macafee, Caroline Urbas; our ever-flexible production manager, Joe Gannon; and, most of all, thanks to our authors: Ula Taylor and Tarika Lewis, who delivered an invaluable, historical work that will have meaning for many years to come; Melvin Van Peebles, for remembering old friends and introducing us to new ones, especially his son, Mario, a passionate, talented, visionary filmmaker, actor, and now author.

CONTENTS

PROLOGUE

BY MELVIN VAN PEEBLES

I remember it well. We were coming from Washington, D.C. or maybe it was just from Philadelphia, anyway the train was hurtling northward through the darkness to New York City.

I sat there glaring out of the train window. I was annoyed, no not annoyed, more than that I was pissed off. Outside, the night had reduced the world to hucksterish billboard ads and points of light whizzing past on a jet black canvas.

My oldest son Mario sat next to me in the aisle seat. I could feel his muscular arm against my shoulder. I should never have bought him that set of weights for his four-teenth birthday, the ungrateful kid, this is the thanks I get. He had just opened the Pandora's box of hope. And frankly I was frightened, frightened of a dream that big.

I shifted my position away from Mario and continued staring out the window. The view didn't help my mood much. Tiny towns alternated with dimly lit country roads. Roads that took God knows who to God knows where. Each village was built to face whatever road there might be. They stood winking and blinking their neon charms at the potential customers whooshing past on the high-way, with their butts/backyards turned toward the railroad tracks…*Good ole American Pragmatism in flagrante delic-to.…* The towns figuring, if you don't bring us business, Mr. Iron-horse/Amtrak, kiss my ass.

We glided past the rear end of some kind of a metal shop. The yard was filled with rusting stacks of rods and racks standing in puddles of purple flourescent water.

For ten years!...that's what I was feeling so huffy about... for ten years I had been working on a novel about the early years of the Black Panther Party. And now this! Now that it was all finished except the final polish.

Since I respected Mario's insight I had shown it to him for comments. And what does my first born tell me.... "Gee, Pop, I think it's great!" So far so good, if only he had stopped there. But then he added, "YOU KNOW IT WOULD MAKE A GREAT MOVIE!"

Voilà! the Pandora's box I was talking about, my wildest dream, my story about the Black Panthers turned into a movie. Of course, the downside of dreaming is the potential for being disappointed... that's what I was frightened and angry about.

You see, I was an early advocate of the Black Panthers. My first American album, "Brer Soul," had only one other thing on its cover outside of my name and the title, and that was "FREE HUEY!" I also used to give benefit con-certs to help raise money for the Panther Party. When my third feature film, *Sweet Sweetback's Baadasssss Song,*

came out, the Party dedicated an entire issue to the film and made it mandatory viewing for all members.

Down through the years, there have been gripping per-sonal accounts of the Panther experience written by indi-vidual members, but what I was striving for was not the personal, not a specific tree, but the forest itself. As fasci-nating as each story was in its own right, I felt that the big picture was even more incredible.

How to do this? I had been wrestling for years with how to capture the sweep, majesty, courage, arrogance, duplicity, and evil. I had felt that as heart-wrenching as the individual memoirs were, the big picture was even more devastating.

Over the years, things happened that aided and abetted my thesis. Through the Freedom of Information Act there were periodic revelations concerning the FBI harassment of the Panthers. A congressional committee admitted that the government had used illegal tactics in its zeal to destroy the Panthers, not to mention that it had been less than candid in its portrayal of the Panthers to the media. However, most of this new information concerning the Panthers never became common knowledge. In the strict sense, it was available to the public, but it was not accessi-ble to the public. I said "most of the information." I con-sider analysis a potent form of information, which I feel was sorely lacking. I had never seen the obvious leap from the government's admitted duplicity and culpability for the rise of drugs. Although the direct correlation between the proliferation of drugs in the black communi-ties and the struggle for liberty had been alluded to in whispers, I had never seen it out in the open.

Anyway, back to the book....Why had I chosen to use a novel to carry my message in the first place? There were three reasons:

ONE, in order to keep the perspective as broad as possi-ble I needed the latitude of the fiction form.

TWO, I also felt fiction was more user-friendly and would probably have a wider readership. Of course, a wider audience might be the kiss of death for the project, which brings me to my last point.

THREE, I felt that a bookish audience would not be seen as such a threat as a movie audience, and I just might be able to get the story into print. I did not know if I would be able to find a publisher courageous enough to make such an incendiary story available to the public.

Here I was wondering if I could even find a book pub-lisher, and my son was suggesting that I should tell my tale via the twentieth century's mass medium par excellence.

I stared at the dilapidated rear ends of the tiny towns whistling past and read the slogans...

REGINA WELDING/ RAHWAY, NEW JERSEY/ DRI-PRINT FOILS/ WALLACE CHEVROLET/ TRENTON MAKES—THE WORLD TAKES/ BENNET HEAT TREATMENT/ MERCK CHIMNEY/ DO NOT CROSS/ GUARANTEED DESTRUCTION OF CONFIDENTIAL RECORDS...

I turned to my son. "I won't water down the truth," I blurted. "Or make political compromises."

"No, Pop, you shouldn't. You gotta tell it just like it is. I didn't know half this stuff. I couldn't put the manuscript down, it's great. It's got everything."

"O.K., if it's so great, let 'em read the book."

"A lot of people don't read all that much."

"Listen, son, no studio would give us the go ahead. Look, I haven't had a directing job since *Sweetback*, not to mention the assassination attempts against me. I don't want the same thing to happen to you. We gave at the office."

"C'mon, Pop. Do a screenplay of the novel."

I went back to the window. The rocking of the train was usually like a soothing lullaby, but it wasn't working. We were crossing the marshlands of New Jersey.... An old Chrysler, its rusted top some indescribable color, like a bad dye job, under the grayish green rays of a security lamp dangling from a pole.... What the hell were the two of them doing sticking out of the middle of some scummy lake...and why the hell was I even listening to my son at all...why the hell do poor colored, no make that negro, no make that black, no make that afro...no African Americans always end up having to be the yeast in the bread of democracy anyway?

I turned back to Mario. "I'll never be able to pull it off by myself."

"You won't have to. We'll produce it together," he promised. "I'm with you all the way, Pop."

And Mario kept his promise.

Later we brought in another brother we could trust, Preston Holmes, and together, a zillion ups and downs and narrow escapes later, the three of us had pulled it off.

Normally, when I do a project, I write myself little essays from time to time about what I hope to achieve and about what I have in mind as a precaution in case I lose my bearings in the fray of creativity. If my advice to myself was good enough for the book, it was good enough for the movie, too. Here are a few brief excerpts from various notes I had written to myself, oh so many years ago.

Dear Melvin,
In the beginning the struggle for Civil Rights, equality, freedom, primary citizenship, etc. meant to most American blacks and whites Dr. Martin Luther King Jr.'s original tactic of non-violence. But before he died, the submissiveness implicit in such a strategy was wearing thin to a lot of restless youths in the ghettos of the nation, especially in the urban areas—even to Dr. King himself, a fact largely overlooked in the canonization that followed his assassination. Notwithstanding, there has always been a current in American life that advocates standing up for oneself— from the Boston Tea Party to Nat Turner. A current as American as apple pie or the Fourth of July is to say, "Whoa, there...enough is enough."

Still, in 1966, American tradition or not, the long history of brutality toward blacks or not, it came as a profound shock to see a group of young black men carrying guns, standing on the steps of a California courthouse proclaiming they had founded an organization for Black Self-Defense.

Dear Melvin,
RE: Freedom of Info Act
Facts are coming out...up to a point. There is more to the story than meets the FBI files. "Is," present tense, instead of "was," because America continues to pay a heavy price for its law enforcement's lapse in judgment. The lapse fostered the drug virus in the black community, the very same virus that has grown into a nationwide plague.

PS: Hey Melvin, how did a ragtag posse of dropouts manage to put together a national organization under the nose of the authorities anyhow?

PART 1—THE HISTORY
ULA Y. TAYLOR & J. TARIKA LEWIS

BEGINNINGS

Historians link the modern civil rights movement with World War II. As Americans went off to war against both Japan and Nazi Germany, factories geared themselves for a huge defense buildup. African Americans welcomed war industry employment because they were disproportionately represented among the underpaid and the unemployed. However, when they sought work where employers literally begged for laborers, they were primarily offered low-paid service jobs. Government-financed training programs refused African Americans despite President Franklin Roosevelt's order prohibiting discrimination in war industries.

Many African Americans believed that one could not lay claim to the rights of full-fledged citizenship without participating in the defense of the country. For them, the war was not simply a fight to wear a military uniform and earn money but a struggle for equality in the United States.

When African American soldiers returned home from fighting a "war for democracy," they were more willing to attack lynchings, disfranchisement, white primaries, Jim Crow laws, and separate-but-unequal education. Nonetheless, most of the battles waged by African Americans to remove the vestiges of slavery were short-lived, unconnected demonstrations lacking an overarching theme. Not until the Montgomery, Alabama, bus boycott (1955–56) did an entire African American community mobilize against Jim Crow segregation. Mrs. Rosa Parks refused to give up her bus seat to a white patron and was arrested. Leaders of the black community, led by the Women's Political Council (WPC) and the National Association for the Advancement of Colored People (NAACP), formed the Montgomery Improvement Association and elected the young Martin Luther King, Jr. president. The WPC, three hundred professional African American women, had documented abuses by white bus drivers and run off 50,000 notices to citizens urging them not to ride the buses. For over a year, men, women, and children walked and carpooled until the buses were integrated.

The bus boycott in Montgomery was not the first of its kind. African Americans in Baton Rouge, Tallahassee, and Birmingham had earlier protested against the humiliating segregated bus seating, however, nothing compared to Montgomery. This united front of African Americans captured the attention of the national media. Their protest was dignified and their leaders were charismatic.

The boycotters used as their organizing base the church—one of the few institutions controlled by African Americans. Citizens in Montgomery attended church nightly to receive updated information and spiritual renewal. At the triumphant end of the boycott, the ministers organized into the Southern Christian Leadership Conference (SCLC), which led the way to desegregate the South and "redeem the soul of America." King became the most sought-after spokesperson for the nonviolent movement. Ironically, the most successful nonviolent demonstrations were televised violent assaults by racist whites, water-hosing and setting dogs on black people. King's vision and activism, based on Christian principles, transformed him into the leader of the first phase of the civil rights movement as it developed in the South.

The year 1960 marked the beginning of the decade that ignited the second wave of the struggle. On February 1, four black students from North Carolina Agricultural and Technical College in Greensboro sat down at a Woolworth store lunch counter reserved for whites. The waitress refused to serve them, and they remained seated for 45 minutes until the store closed. Their sit-in was a spontaneous gesture that culminated in an organized protest against Jim Crow. The following day, thirty students joined their protest, and by the end of the week two hundred were involved, including some white students. By the end of February, sit-ins spanned seven southern states and included close to fifty thousand young activists. Continuing the tradition of nonviolent protest, the students were orderly. They learned techniques to protect themselves from physical attacks by whites without retaliating, and they prayed.

SCLC leadership was in awe of the students' bravery and Christian commitment to desegregate the South. Unlike boycotts, sit-ins reeked of civil disobedience. The students were breaking the law and provoking arrests and jail time. SCLC wanted these students to form an auxiliary youth wing to their organization, so in 1960 they sponsored an Easter weekend Youth Leadership Conference at Shaw University in Raleigh, North Carolina. King was the keynote speaker. Ella Baker, SCLC's major female voice, inspired the 140 students in attendance to form their own organization, the Student Nonviolent Coordinating Committee (SNCC). Baker stated, "None of the great leadership had anything to do with the sit-ins starting. [They] spread, to a large extent, because of…the young enthusiasm and the need for action." By June, SNCC published the first edition of its newspaper, *Student Voice*. The most committed activists left college and became full-time "field secretaries." Under the guidance of Baker, SNCC flourished into a major civil rights organization.

The Congress of Racial Equality (CORE), formed during World War II, entered the student fray by daring to desegregate interstate bus travel with the freedom rides in 1961. On May 4, James Farmer

Previous page: **D**emonstrators at the August 28, 1963 March on Washington.

Below: **Dr. Martin Luther King, Jr.'s family and supporters prepare to welcome Dr. King back to Atlanta from a stay in prison, October 1960.**

At right: **Demonstrators at the March on Washington.**

led volunteers from Washington, D.C., into the Deep South via Greyhound bus, with the goal of receiving service at segregated terminal facilities. If arrested for civil disobedience, the activists refused bail in hopes of placing pressure on the jail system. Freedom rides pushed the nonviolent direct-action principle to another level. Expert organization and long-term commitment on behalf of the activists were imperative for the riders to succeed. CORE demanded police protection from hostile whites, who beat activists as they departed from buses. After CORE discontinued the freedom rides, SNCC revived the campaign on May 23. SNCC activist Diane Nash recalled that prior to boarding buses, "Several made out wills. A few more gave me sealed letters to be mailed if they were killed. Some told me frankly that they were afraid, but they knew this was something that they must do because freedom was worth it."

Freedom rides brought the entire nation into the struggle. Boycotts were local, sit-ins were regional, but freedom rides encompassed the whole nation. They attacked more complicated problems that required federal intervention. Freedom rides led to the desegregation of bus terminals, but only after vehement attacks on the participants.

The civil rights movement included a hodgepodge of political, educational, and legal issues. Many Americans believed that the movement was over after President Lyndon Johnson on August 6, 1965, signed into law the Voting Rights Act, which guaranteed to all, regardless of color, the right to vote. What else could African Americans want? White America was shocked when Watts, a predominantly black district of Los Angeles, erupted in rebellion from August 11 to 16 five days later. Less than a year later SNCC called for Black Power.

On June 6, 1966, James Meredith, the first African American to attend the University of Mississippi, was shot on the second day of his one-man March Against Fear through Mississippi. SNCC, SCLC, and CORE completed the march on his behalf. SNCC activist Stokely Carmichael led the chant for Black Power at this march. The slogan had multiple meanings. Carmichael argued that Black Power was a call "for black people in this country to unite, to recognize their heritage, to build a sense of community…. It is a call to reject the racist institutions and values of this society."

Although Black Power transformed the civil rights struggle to its next stage, the message was not new. In fact, Malcolm X was the most articulate voice for black empowerment during the 1960s. Malcolm X, spokesperson and minister for the Nation of Islam, was critical of the "nonviolent direct action" civil rights strategy. How could individuals not defend themselves in the midst of a violent onslaught? African Americans had the right to defend themselves against racist acts "by any means necessary." Malcolm articulated the sentiments of many African Americans, particularly those living in northern cities. If citizens did not have the money to sit at a lunch counter or attend college, they were somewhat detached from the victories. Malcolm's message drew thousands into the Nation under the leadership of the Honorable Elijah Muhammad. Malcolm believed that Muhammad "in every aspect of his existence was the

Left: **D**r. Martin Luther King, Jr. leads civil rights workers in prayer after 250 of them were arrested in Selma, Alabama, February 1, 1965.

Below: Stokely Carmichael handing out leaflets outside the Atlanta induction center after one of his SNCC colleagues refused to be inducted into the army.

At bottom: Carmichael, right, and H. Rap Brown, center, of SNCC in Nashville, May 1967.

Below: **Martin Luther King, Jr., left, with Malcolm X.**

At bottom: **Malcolm X addresses a crowd in Manhattan in August 1963.**

Opposite: **Malcolm, center, with Ahmed Shukairi, left, head of the newly formed Palestine Liberation Organization.**

symbol of moral, mental, and spiritual reform among American black people." Malcolm followed Messenger Muhammad's teachings until he learned about his involvement in extramarital liaisons. After Malcolm met with the Messenger in April 1963 about his affairs, Malcolm was suspended and subsequently ousted from the Nation. Malcolm regrouped and founded the Organization for Afro-American Unity (OAAU), a political, secular organization. Many African Americans, especially northern urbanites, embraced Malcolm as their leader and joined the OAAU. Malcolm's life teachings were widely disseminated through his autobiography published in 1965. Activists digested his words, which inspired them to demand power to control their communities and culturally transform the old order in the United States. Malcolm's assassination on February 21, 1965, devastated African Americans. His legacy propelled two young men, Huey P. Newton and Bobby Seale, to carry on his ideas.

Oakland, California, is north of the Berkeley border and eight miles west of the San Francisco-Oakland Bay Bridge. The vast majority of African Americans in Oakland migrated to the city from the South to work in the defense industries. Between 1940 and 1960 the total population in the Bay Area almost doubled. The 1940 census reported 19,759 African Americans, two-thirds in Alameda County, specifically Oakland. By 1960 the number had expanded to 238,754.

As with most cities, residential segregation was alive and well in the Bay Area. Unemployment rates were high. But African Americans' were four times higher than whites'. An African American with education equal to that of a white Oaklander stood more than a one-and-a-half greater chance of being unemployed.

These conditions made the experiences of African Americans and whites vastly different in Oakland. It was hard for whites to imagine the level of police brutality that African Americans complained about. They were not alone. A 1966 Gallup poll found that 35 percent of African American men believed there was police brutality in their community; only 7 percent of whites agreed. In 1966, a U.S. Senate survey in Watts found that 60 percent of African American youth believed that there was police brutality; half said they had actually witnessed and experienced it firsthand.

The Oakland police department was an extension of the racist South that African Americans had fled. Many officers were recruited from Mississippi. In 1966, 96 percent of the police department was white, while 45 to 50 percent of the population it served was not. Not surprisingly, 98.5 percent of the higher-ranking positions (sergeant and above) were white men. Because police brutality was frequent and volatile, African Americans sought an independent civilian review board. The Oakland City Council and Police Chief Charles Gains were not responsive to their efforts. Gains told African Americans to submit their written complaints to white officers in the Oakland Internal Affairs Section. It was up to the victim to prove police harassment. In response, a citizen stated, "They catch you in an alley and beat you up. How you gonna prove it? You got some bruises on you? You got drunk and fell down? You got shot? You resisted arrest." Huey Newton and Bobby Seale identified with the predicament and pledged to organize and mobilize African Americans to stop police brutality in their community.

BLACK PANTHER PARTY

Many African Americans in the South moved North during the war. Huey P. Newton's family migrated from Monroe, Louisiana, to Oakland in 1945, so that his father could work in the war industries. The family moved around, and Huey attended several grammar and junior high schools. In junior high he could not read. He wrote, "At that time, and earlier, I associated reading with being an adult: when I became an adult, I would automatically be able to read, too." Not until Huey's high school senior year did he learn to read. He was too embarrassed to ask for help, but taught himself by using his brother Melvin's poetry books. Melvin often read poetry aloud, and Huey remembered what he heard. Huey associated the "sounds" in his head with "the words on the page." After months, he finally "knew [his] way through a book." Huey writes that "during those long years in the Oakland public schools, I did not have one teacher who taught me anything relevant to my own life experience." By 1959 Huey not only earned his "farce" high school diploma from Oakland Technical High School but also a reputation as a fighter.

In fall 1959, Newton enrolled in Merritt College in Oakland. Though a college student, Newton still ran with the "brothers on the block," and any money he had "had come from petty crime…." One day, while expressing his frustrations about the mass oppression inflicted on African Americans, his fraternity brothers responded that he "sounded like a guy named Donald Warden."

Warden, a graduate of Boalt Hall Law School at UC Berkeley, was the head of the Afro-American Association. Warden rented a storefront across the street from Merritt College and initiated self-help programs including Economic Night where solutions and strategies for empowerment were discussed. Warden created "James Brown Stamps" that were used at businesses throughout the community. To most Oaklanders, Warden was viewed as revolutionary, a man ahead of his time, because he used the term "Afro-American." Newton started attending the association meetings, which were also reading groups filled with college stu-

Previous page: **H**uey P. Newton, Black Panther Party Minister of Defense.

Above: **Bobby Seale, chairman of the Black Panther Party.**

dents. They read W.E.B. DuBois's *The Soul of Black Folks*, Ralph Ellison's *Invisible Man*, and James Baldwin's *The Fire Next Time*. Huey enjoyed reading about black history and culture. On the weekends the group took to the streets and spoke on corners about racism in America. During the October 1962 Cuban missile crisis, the Afro-American Association members debated Merritt College students.

Bobby Seale witnessed Huey's philosophical attack and was impressed by his ability to explain complex issues. Seale, six years Newton's senior, had attended Merritt College part-time while he worked on the Gemini missile project, beginning in late 1958. Seale initially majored in engineering but was soon engaged in the study of African history and culture. By 1962, Bobby already had a desire to go to Africa, and after hearing Newton rap about African and American history, he knew that he wanted to join the association. Seale discusses in his autobiography how the brothers greeted each other with the new soul handshake and he soon "wanted to imitate Donald Warden's snappy, boppy, hip gestures and overemphasis. I even asked him could I speak. I found I could hold the attention of a crowd with my own boppy gestures."

Seale and Newton attracted folks from the North Oakland neighborhood to the association. Warden was excited to have their participation, but Huey felt he wanted the brothers on the block to serve as his bodyguards. Sometimes the association's street debates turned into confrontations. Even worse Newton wrote that he witnessed Warden bow down to the Oakland City Council, and heard Warden say that black people needed to get off welfare and stop collecting unemployment checks.

Seale was in the Afro-American Association for only two months before Huey left. Newton was thankful for the opportunity to learn about black history, "but I could not accept Warden's refusal to deal with the Black present."

Huey was amazed that he really enjoyed the learning process in college. He slowly transformed intellectually from a nationalist to a socialist. He studied with Marxists and attend Progressive Labor Party meetings. After reading four volumes by Chinese Communist leader Mao Zedong* his conversion was complete. Yet he still searched for answers to racial questions. After reading C. Eric Lincoln's *Black Muslims in America,* he became fascinated with Malcolm X.

He heard Malcolm speak at a conference sponsored by the Afro-American Association at McClymonds High School in Oakland. He was so impressed that he irregularly attended Muslim mosques in both Oakland and San Francisco. In the San Francisco mosque, Newton started "processing" for his "X" and became acquainted with Messenger Muhammad's ten point program. Activities within the mosque were extremely restrictive and required complete submission to Islamic beliefs. But having grown up in a deeply religious family, Newton "had had enough of religion and could not bring [himself] to adopt another one."

Huey once again was on the search for an organization when he found out that his college peers Kenny and Carol Freeman, Isaac Moore, Max Stanford, Doug Allen, Ernie Allen, and Alex Papillion had formed a West Coast branch of the Revolutionary Action

Movement (RAM), which sponsored lectures, films, slide shows, dances and musical events. Bobby Seale was already a member and invited Newton to attend a meeting. Newton recalled that RAM claimed to be an underground movement to overthrow the federal government, but in reality, they were people who wrote a lot and indulged in talk, not action. Huey was impatient with their cautiousness.

Newton continued to socialize with the neighborhood brothers, an experience that convinced him that he did not have the same desires as the college group. Huey wanted freedom from material possessions and debt, but he often heard others express their need for fancy cars and houses. Keeping one foot in the community and the other on campus, Huey soon merged the two. Because the police were often harassing and brutalizing black people, Huey began to study political science and the rights of citizens to defend themselves.

After graduating from Merritt College, he enrolled in San Francisco Law School—not to become a lawyer but to stop police harassment and "to become a better burglar." Huey feared that all of his petty crime would eventually catch up with him. He intensely studied the California penal code, focusing on ambiguous areas. Often arrested, he would be released with no charge. Finally, in 1964, Huey's luck ran out when he was convicted of assault against Odell Lee, an Oakland brother. Huey had stabbed him at a party. He was sentenced to six months and spent his first month in the "soul breaker" hole of solitary confinement at Alameda County jail.

Newton was released in 1965 and soon looked up his old friend Bobby Seale, who had left RAM, a short-lived underground movement. Former RAM members organized the Soul Students Advisory Council (SSAC) at Merritt College and the Black Panther Party of Northern California. Huey joined the SSAC central committee, which also included Doug Allen, Bobby Seale, Isaac Moore, Virtual Murrell, and Alex Papillion. The SSAC organized a major rally against the draft of black men into the Vietnam War and also led a successful protest to have a black history course added to the curriculum at Merritt College.

Their activities attracted many new members and no longer was SSAC indirectly controlled by RAM. SSAC's augmented membership allowed them to take on an explosive issue, the creation of an African American studies program. Newton and Seale hoped to advance SSAC's agenda by encouraging students to wear guns in front of the school. Huey said, "Partly, the rally would express our opposition to police brutality, but it would also intimidate the authorities at City College who were resisting our program." Huey and Bobby's suggestion was flatly rejected by the SSAC. Nevertheless, during this time neither Newton nor Seale considered creating an organization of their own.

When the Watts riots exploded in 1965, it revealed that black urbanites rejected Dr. Martin Luther King's nonviolent posture. Oakland police began to carry shotguns to further their intimidation tactics. The times were changing, and Newton and Seale were in tune. Newton, Seale, and Gerald Horton (Weasel) heard about the citizen alert patrols in Watts. In radio-equipped cars the Temporary

BABY OF REVOLUTION

Beautiful black baby
  Wrapped in innocent love
Beautiful black baby
  Knows not of an unjust world

Beautiful black baby
  Your daddy has gone to war
Beautiful black baby
  He's fighting, and here we are

Beautiful black baby
  Daddy loves us so
Beautiful black baby
  He had no choice: but to go

Beautiful black baby
  There's news pigs killed your
  dad
Beautiful black baby
  Freedom and peace we
    never had…

WHAT WE WANT

1. We want freedom, we want power to determine the destiny of our black community.

2. We want full employment for our people.

3. We want an end to the robbery by the white man of our black community.

4. We want decent housing, fit for shelter of human beings.

5. We want education for our people that exposes the true nature of this decadent American society. We want education that teaches us our true history and our role in this present day society.

6. We want all black men to be exempt from military service.

7. We want an immediate end to police brutality and murder of black people.

8. We want freedom for all black men held in federal, state, county, and city prisons and jails.

9. We want all black people when brought to trial to be tried in court by a jury of their peer group or people from their black communities, as defined by the constitution of the United States.

10. We want land, bread, housing, education, clothing, justice and peace.

Alliance of Local Organizations, members of various civil rights groups, cruised South Central Los Angeles monitoring police radio calls and driving to troubled locations to observe police conduct. Each car had a white handkerchief tied to its radio antenna to identify it. The citizens' purpose was "to collect, analyze, and channel to responsible citizen groups and social agencies, accurate reports growing out of charges of police misbehavior, brutality and harassment, unequal enforcement and application under the law." The Temporary Alliance members also educated individuals on their rights and obligations under the law. The citizen alert patrols were short-lived due to the ruthless Los Angeles Police Department, which lashed out against this activity.

On the evening of March 17, 1966, Seale, Huey, and Weasel ventured to Berkeley to purchase blues records but eventually found themselves in a confrontation with local police in front of the Forum, a sidewalk cafe where intellectuals and hippies gathered. Huey, who really appreciated Bobby's ability to communicate, asked him to recite his poem "Uncle Sammy Call Me Full of Lucifer." Seale drew a crowd of listeners, and soon a uniformed cop told him he was under arrest for using profanity and blocking the sidewalk. After Bobby stated that he had a right to free speech, officers began to tug and pull at him. Huey stepped in, and the fight was on. Both Seale and Newton were arrested.

The level of police violence in the Bay Area seemed to be increasing daily. On March 29, 1966, a black man was shot seven times in the back by an Oakland officer and left paralyzed. In San Francisco, on the same day, Matthew Johnson, a sixteen-year-old African American youth accused of car theft, was shot to death by a local officer. Huey Newton knew that their time had come to organize black people into a politically astute vanguard, so they could confront the political establishment that kept black citizens living in deplorable conditions and allowed police officers to harass and murder them.

Seale and Newton conversed about politics, social problems, and the strengths and weaknesses of other progressive organizations. Most of these conversations took place at Seale's apartment, close to the campus. Others participated in the discussions, that became heated, because there were so many issues and so few solutions. They read Frantz Fanon, Mao Zedong, and Che Guevara, and studied Malcolm X's writings and speeches. Robert Williams's *Negroes with Guns* and literature on the Deacons of Defense had a profound affect on the Party's development. Newton writes that "in a sense, these sessions at Bobby's house were our political education classes, and the Party sort of grew out of them."

By spring 1966, Seale and Newton "were testing ideas that would capture the imagination of the community" they wanted to serve. They talked to brothers about their rights as citizens, which included the right to bear arms. Because Seale worked at the government Antipoverty Center, which gave legal advice, Huey also had access to their law library. During the summer months, Seale and Newton circulated within the black neighborhoods of Oakland, Berkeley, Richmond, and San Francisco, talking with the folks about their constitutional right to have weapons. Brothers and sisters could identify with what Huey and Bobby were saying, because they had experienced and witnessed so much outlaw behavior by the police. Police harassment was not unique to Oakland. By the end of the summer, forty-three northern cities went up in smoke, and more than thirty-five hundred people were arrested throughout the nation. Most of these rebellions were ignited by violent police confrontation with black citizens.

The summer of 1966 had a profound impact on American youth. When students returned to school in September, many formed study groups and Black Student Unions (BSUs) to find out what had deliberately been kept secret—African historical truth, traditions, culture, and language, as well as recognition of African Americans' accomplishments. Bobby Seale tapped into this fever and organized a successful Negro History Fact group. These BSUs, led by Oakland Technical High, became the training grounds for many future Panthers.

One afternoon in October, Huey and Bobby went to the government Antipoverty Center and reviewed all the books they had read. None fit their circumstances; a "unique situation required a unique program." So, Huey started to dictate to Seale his thoughts about the essential aspects of any program that was to address the survival of oppressed people. It only took twenty minutes to write the ten-point program, which they patterned after the Nation of Islam's platform. They gave their written notes to Melvin Newton to proofread for grammatical errors. Then the cofounders asked Seale's wife, Artie, and Newton's girlfriend, LaVerne Williams to type the final version.

They named their organization the Black Panther Party for Self-Defense, taking the lead from the Lowndes County Freedom Organization (LCFO), an independent political party in Alabama that had selected as its emblem a black panther. John Hulett, LCFO chairman, stated, "The black panther is an animal that when it is pres-

"THE BLACK PANTHER IS AN ANIMAL THAT WHEN IT IS PRESSURED IT MOVES BACK UNTIL IT IS CORNERED, THEN COMES OUT FIGHTING FOR LIFE OR DEATH".

BLACK PANTHER

Words & Music through LEN H. CHANDLER JR.
© 1966 Len H. Chandler Jr.

Black sheep in the coun-try, Black sheep in the town, No sheep ev-en has a

half a chance with so—man-y wolf a-round. You'd better walk with the black pan-

ther, That's all that ya got-ta do, 'Cause when you're walk-in' with the

Big Black Cat no wolves 'll be run-nin' you.—

WHAT WE BELIEVE

1. We believe that black people will not be free until we are able to determine our destiny.

2. We believe that the federal government is responsible and obligated to give every man employment or a guaranteed income. We believe that if the white American business men will not give full employment, then the means of production should be taken from the business men and placed in the community so that the people of the community can organize and employ all of its people and give a high standard of living....

7. We believe we can end police brutality in our black community by organizing black self defense groups that are dedicated to defending our black community from racist police oppression and brutality. The Second Amendment of the Constitution of the United States gives us a right to bear arms. We therefore believe that all black people should arm themselves for self defense. . . .

10. We hold these truths to be self-evident, that all men are created equal, they are endowed by their creator with certain inalienable rights, that among these are life, liberty and the pursuit of happiness. . . .whenever any form of government becomes destructive of these ends, it is the right of people to alter or to abolish it, and to institute new government, laying its foundation on such principles and organizing its powers in such form as to them shall seem most likely to effect their safety and happiness....

Right: **A** group of Panthers in formation, wearing their distinctive uniforms.

sured it moves back until it is cornered, then it comes out fighting for life or death. We felt we had been pushed back long enough and that it was time for Negroes to come out and take over." Huey became the minister of defense and Bobby the chairman. Huey wanted Seale to be the formal chairman because he had excellent communication skills and organizing experience. Seale would conduct the meetings and execute the administrative workings of the Party.

The Party officially began on October 15, 1966. Sixteen-year-old Bobby James Hutton became the first male volunteer and Party treasurer. He was affectionately nicknamed Lil' Bobby. Seale had been Hutton's youth counselor and later got him a job at the Antipoverty Center. Hutton helped circulate the copies of the ten-point program and "articulate" the Party's agenda. During the recruitment period, the threesome clarified that the Party was not racist. On the contrary, it opposed all forms of racism, especially when institutionalized to benefit capitalists.

With their program intact, the next phase was implementation. They selected point No. 7—an immediate end to police brutality and murder of black people—as the community's most urgent issue. First, they had to obtain guns for self-defense. In November 1966, they convinced a radical Japanese brother, Richard M. Aoki, to give them two guns—a shotgun and a pistol. They began to patrol in December, and Seale recounts how fearless Newton was when they encountered the police. In front of the first Party office that opened January 1, 1967, Huey was asked by a police officer, "What are you doing with the guns?" Huey responded, "What are you doing with your gun?" The officer asked Huey for his phone number, and Newton responded, "The Fifth Amendment. You ever heard of it? Don't you know about the constitutional right of a person not to testify against himself? Five! I don't have to give you anything but my identification, name, address so therefore I don't even want to talk to you. You can leave my car and leave me alone. I don't even want to hear you." Huey and Bobby won the brothers over, and their numbers grew. So did the need for more guns.

Huey devised a means to earn money and develop the philosophical component of the Party's agenda. Seale and Newton purchased cartons of *Quotations from Chairman Mao* ("The Little Red Book") from a vendor in San Francisco's Chinatown. The books cost the Party thirty cents each. They sold them for one dollar at the University of California, Berkeley. Seale and Newton recognized that the advocates of the free speech movement at Berkeley craved material that substantiated their philosophical standpoint. With Lil' Bobby Hutton, they positioned themselves in front of Sather Gate, sold all the Red Books, and made a $170 profit. In a few days they had earned approximately $850. They purchased more guns.

The Panthers patrolled Oakland, Richmond, Berkeley, and San Francisco. Huey's childhood friend, David Hilliard, wrote that after his first Panther patrol, "his mind and heart" had "been captured." Huey and Bobby made it clear to all brothers to be prepared to do battle if a policeman drew his gun. "We'd shoot it out and let these jive simple-minded racist police know where it's at!" Newton warned his comrades that "once it starts...we may wind up dead or

in prison." Without a doubt these young men had to overcome or suppress the life-threatening reality associated with the patrols. It took courage to police the police. Cops killed black people in cold blood and called it "justifiable homicide."

Huey wanted to ensure that black residents viewed their patrols as helpful to the community. He didn't want people to see the Panthers as thuggish, gun-toting brothers without an organized agenda. He came up with the idea that all Panthers should wear a neat, polished uniform—black slacks, ironed powder-blue shirts, black tie or turtleneck, black leather sports jacket. Their signature black berets were a result of Huey and Bobby watching a movie about the resistance by the French underground to the Nazis. The French wore berets; they liked what they saw. So Panthers wore their berets, tilted to the right

side. By the late 1960s the Panther uniform, especially the leather jackets and berets, became the "revolutionary" fashion statement for many, many people.

The Panthers' armed patrols were random and linked with their daily movements throughout the communities. They would observe police officers questioning black people, inform black citizens of their rights, and offer their services to people who needed a witness in a suit against the officer who harassed them. They were careful to keep their patrols within the bounds of the law, and this infuriated the officers even more. Police brutality against black citizens was reduced. The Panthers confused but never cursed officers, despite police insults hurled at them.

In Huey's efforts to empower black people by reducing their fear, he knew he had to redefine the vessel of their harassment—the police. He sought a word that would not only raise the consciousness of black men and women but also force the officers themselves to reexamine their outlaw role in black communities. Huey first used the word "dog," but it did not become popular. Other words tried included brute, beast, and animal. Then one day he saw on a postcard with the slogan "Support Your Local Police" a small picture of a slobbering pig on the sheriff's star. Huey knew right away that "pig" would do the trick. The Panthers soon began calling police officers pigs, swine, hogs, sows.

Huey's philosophical training in college exposed him to the scholarship of A. J. Ayer, who wrote that "Nothing can be real if it cannot be conceptualized, articulated, and shared." This had a tremendous impact on Newton's thinking. The ideology of the Party was based on this premise. Party rhetoric such as "All Power to the People" and the concept of the "pig" were not spontaneously introduced into the Party's ideology but were calculated choices. The police attempt to intimidate the Panthers and turn the community against them had an opposite impact. The community was proud to

Above: **E**ldridge Cleaver, Black Panther Minister of Information.

Below: **Huey P. Newton, right, with Bobby Seale.**

see young black men defend their rights and stand up to the establishment. Their reputation as fearless freedom fighters grew.

In 1967, Eldridge Cleaver along with Marvin Jackman, Ed Bullins, and Willie Dale founded the Black House in San Francisco. It was an informal cultural center that sponsored poetry readings, jam sessions, and political debates. The Black House with other organizations initiated at Hunter's Point, a predominantly black community in San Francisco, Malcolm X Commemoration Day, featuring Malcolm's widow, Betty Shabazz. Cleaver, like many black urbanites, wanted to revive Malcolm's OAAU.

The San Francisco and Oakland Panthers served as escorts for Shabazz, who was scheduled to speak at the rally and be interviewed by Cleaver for Ramparts Press, publisher of *Ramparts* magazine. Huey made it plain at a meeting before the rally that his Oakland group believed that political and military aspects of the liberation struggle were intertwined. "Politics is war without bloodshed and war is a continuation of politics with bloodshed."

On the day of the rally, seven Oakland Panthers strapped with heavy firepower went to the San Francisco airport to meet Betty Shabazz. The Panthers escorted Shabazz directly to the San Francisco *Ramparts* magazine office. After her interview with Cleaver, a confrontation between the Panthers and the police ensued. Shabazz told Huey that she did not want any pictures taken. When reporter Chuck Banks pushed Huey in the chest, Huey retaliated by knocking Banks out. Cleaver was impressed by Huey's physical resistance and his sheer will and militant determination. A major rift developed between the San Francisco and Oakland activists after this incident.

Left: **B**etty Shabazz, in the dark coat, widow of Malcolm X.

BLACK PANTHER PARTY
NATICNAL HEADQUARTERS
===BERKELEY CALIFORNIA===

NATIONAL CENTRAL COMMITTEE

MINISTER OF DEFENSE. . . . . .HUEY P. NEWTON

CHAIRMAN. . . . . .BOBBY GEORGE SEALE

MINISTER OF INFORMATION. . . . . .LEROY ELDRIDGE CLEAVER

DEPUTY MINISTER OF INFORMATION. . .FRANK JONES

CHIEF OF STAFF. . . . . .DAVID HILLIARD

COMMUNICATION SEC.	FIELD MARSHALS	MINISTER OF EDUCATION	PRIME MINISTER	MINISTER OF JUSTICE	MINISTER OF FOREIGN AFFAIRS	MINISTER OF RELIGION	MINISTER OF CULTURE	MINISTER OF FINANCE

The Oakland chapter was an above-ground armed vanguard, while the Black Panther Party of Northern California was to remain underground to avoid getting totally wiped out. A confrontation between Oakland and San Francisco Panthers occurred at a house party sponsored by the San Francisco group. Oakland Panthers fired shots, but there were no injuries. Huey demanded the group merge, drop their name, or be wiped out. The Northern California group refused the merger, dropped the name, and went on to successfully institute the first Black Studies Department in the country at Merritt College.

Eldridge Cleaver became the minister of information for the Oakland Panthers because of his writing skills and interest in communication. He wrote that he "found harmony" in working with his wife, Kathleen, who served as the Party's communication secretary. Cleaver gave his first speech on April 15, 1967, at Kezar Stadium, San Francisco, criticizing the United States' role in the Vietnam War. Some excerpts of his speech were televised, which caused the state to attempt to revoke his parole and return him to prison. His parole agents advised him to "cool it and forsake my rights in the interest of not antagonizing those in Sacramento who did not like my politics." After consulting with his attorneys, Cleaver decided to avoid these

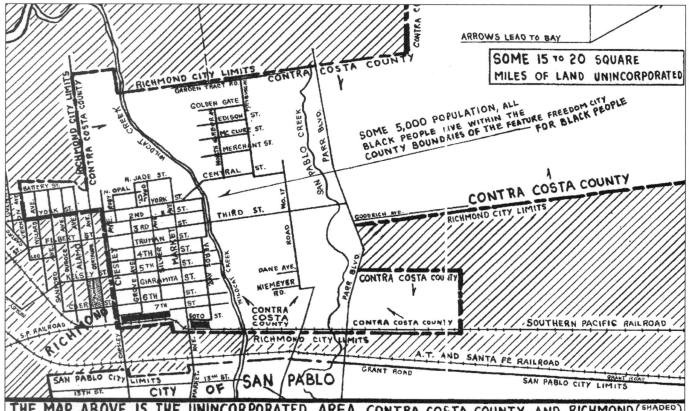

THE MAP ABOVE IS THE UNINCORPORATED AREA, CONTRA COSTA COUNTY, AND RICHMOND (SHADED AREA)

BROTHERS AND SISTERS IF YOU READ POINT NO. 1 OF THE PROGRAM OF THE BLACK PANTHER PARTY FOR SELF DEFENSE UNDER 'WHAT WE WANT NOW!' IT READS: "WE WANT FREEDOM. WE WANT POWER TO DETERMINE THE DESTINY OF OUR BLACK COMMUNITY." IF WE BLACK PEOPLE GET TOGETHER IN THIS COMMUNITY, OUR BLACK COMMUNITY AND INCORPORATE AS A SIX CLASS CITY (and it only takes 5,000 POPULATION. A 5,000 POPULATION EXISTS NOW) WE CAN HAVE OUR OWN POLICE DEPT., OUR OWN COURT, OUR OWN CITY COUNCIL. WE CAN HAVE CO-OP MARKETS, SHOPPING CENTERS, AND COOPERATIVE HOUSING THATS DECENT WITH LOW RENT. WE CAN MAKE JOBS FOR OUR PEOPLE, OUR OWN MAYOR

warnings and continued to exercise his right to free speech.

In April 1967, the Dowell family of North Richmond solicited the Panthers' support. Denzil Dowell (22) had been killed by a Contra Costa County sheriff's deputy on April 1, 1967. Denzil's family knew that the sheriff's report explaining the murder was bogus. Deputies stated that he had been shot three times, but the coroner's report documented six bullets. Several were in his armpits, indicating that his hands were held above his head. Dowell was charged with running and scaling a wall after "being caught in the act of burglary." In truth, he had a debilitating hip injury that prevented his running. The coroner also stated that death was due to bleeding, but there was no blood at the location of his body, implying that he had been moved. The Dowells were refused the right to take photos of Denzil's body, nor were his clothes returned to them. The Panthers investigated the shooting scene and questioned residents about what they heard and saw. The Dowell family had already collected twelve hundred signatures on a petition to call for a grand jury investigation, but nothing had been done. Denzil's brother, George, joined the Party, and his front lawn became the site of rallies. The Panthers initiated an all-out attack on the racism that permeated the community. They patrolled the streets and the schools where white teachers were hitting black children. They also organized the community to confront the sheriff collectively to investigate the killing.

On April 19, 1967, Panthers and community representatives were refused entrance into the sheriff's office with their guns. Huey agreed to remove the guns, because he wanted to exhaust all legal avenues in an attempt to find out what exactly happened to Denzil. The sheriff refused all suggestions by the Panthers and concerned citizens. A deputy stated, "I don't know why you're so upset. This is the first death we've had in the county." He then told the Panthers, "If you people want the policy changed you should go through the legislature." Newton, Seale, Cleaver, and two other Panthers collectively agreed to take his advice.

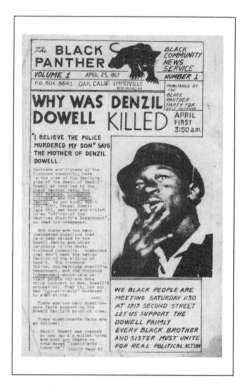

Top: **T**ommie Smith, center, and John Carlos give the Black Power salute after winning medals in the 200-meter run at the 1968 Olympic Games in Mexico City.

Below: **The front page of the first issue of** *The Black Panther*

SACRAMENTO

L ike most state capitals, Sacramento was a bureaucratic nightmare. The Black Panthers and the Dowell family were under no illusions that they could change laws in one day or even effectively pressure the establishment to reopen Denzil's murder investigation. The Panthers elected to mount an attack on Republican assemblyman Don Mulford's bill that aimed to ban the display of loaded weapons within incorporated areas. The bill would make the Panthers' patrols illegal, despite the Second Amendment to the U.S. Constitution, which guarantees the right to bear arms. The Panthers wanted the country to understand that the premise behind the bill was to take away the rights of black people.

Newton wanted to go with the Panther group to Sacramento, but Seale and others voted him down for several reasons. First, they feared for his life. Second, at this time, police officials did not have a good grasp of the actual numbers of Panthers. By leaving a leader at home, the Panthers could keep the officers guessing. Third, the fact that Newton was still on probation after the Odell Lee case meant that he could be incarcerated for an extended period if he were arrested again. Finally, if arrests were made, someone needed to be on the outside to orchestrate releases.

Newton sent the entourage to Sacramento with specific instructions to Bobby to fire back if fired upon. They were to "use whatever means necessary to defend" themselves. He also told them not to resist an arrest as long as they had delivered their message. He told Bobby not to enter the Capitol but to read the message to the press from the steps. Huey concluded by telling Lil' Bobby to stay close to Chairman Seale.

On May 2, 1967, Seale led a group of thirty Panthers and their supporters to the capitol. Twenty of the twenty-four men were armed; Artie, Bobby's wife, was one of six women present. They walked toward the capitol building in a nonmilitary, dispersed manner. Governor Ronald Reagan was speaking to a group of two hundred Future Youth Leaders on the lawn and was startled by what he

EXECUTIVE MANDATE NO.1

Below is the statement prepared by Huey P. Newton, Minister of Defense, and delivered by Bobby Seale, Chairman of the Black Panther Party for Self-Defense, May 2, 1967, at the state capitol in Sacramento, California. . . .

THE BLACK PANTHER PARTY FOR SELF-DEFENSE CALLS UPON THE AMERICAN PEOPLE IN GENERAL, AND THE BLACK PEOPLE IN PARTICULAR TO TAKE CAREFUL NOTE OF THE RACIST CALIFORNIA LEGISLATURE WHICH IS NOW CONSIDERING LEGISLATION AIMED AT KEEPING THE BLACK PEOPLE DISARMED AND POWERLESS AT THE VERY SAME TIME THAT RACIST POLICE AGENCIES THROUGHOUT THE COUNTRY ARE INTENSIFYING THE TERROR, BRUTALITY, MURDER AND REPRESSION OF BLACK PEOPLE. . . .

THE BLACK PANTHER PARTY FOR SELF-DEFENSE BELIEVES THAT THE TIME HAS COME FOR BLACK PEOPLE TO ARM THEMSELVES AGAINST THIS TERROR BEFORE IT IS TOO LATE. THE PENDING MULFORD ACT BRINGS THE HOUR OF DOOM ONE STEP NEARER. A PEOPLE WHO HAVE SUFFERED SO MUCH FOR SO LONG AT THE HANDS OF A RACIST SOCIETY MUST DRAW THE LINE SOMEWHERE. WE BELIEVE THAT THE BLACK COMMUNITIES OF AMERICA MUST RISE UP AS ONE MAN TO HALT THE PROGRESSION OF A TREND THAT LEADS INEVITABLY TO THEIR TOTAL DESTRUCTION.

saw. Reporters, police, and cameramen who were covering the Reagan story swarmed around the Panthers. Somehow, amid all the commotion, Seale was able to fulfill the Party's Sacramento goal. He read the Party's message to the people, Executive Mandate No.1.

A reporter then asked Seale if the Panthers were going inside the capitol to the Assembly. Bobby remembered Huey's instructions, but he was also curious. On the spot he made the decision to enter the capitol. Everyone stepped aside and cleared a path for the Panthers. Some observers muttered, "Niggers with guns, niggers with guns." Scholar Reginald Major writes that legislatures had "witnessed sit-ins, sleep-ins, pray-ins, and other protest activities," but "they were all eclipsed…when the Panthers held a gun-in."

Bobby tried to locate the place where citizens observe the legislative sessions. Following the directions of reporters, the Panthers soon found themselves on the floor of the Assembly and not in the balcony observation gallery. As they filed out, officers tried to confiscate their weapons. Bobby Hutton got into an argument with a police officer who had latched onto his arm. Hutton asked, "Am I under arrest? Am I under arrest? Then let go of my arm." As they departed from the capitol, Seale once again read Mandate No.1 to the reporters.

Once the Panthers reached their cars, they were exhausted from the Sacramento heat but in a hurry to get back to Oakland. It did not take long for one of the older cars to run hot. Seale hesitantly stopped at a gas station for water to cool the engine. Sacramento police—responding to a false rumor that an officer inside the capitol had been assaulted—quickly surrounded and arrested them at the station.

Twenty-four men were charged with conspiracy, carrying concealed weapons, brandishing a weapon in a threatening manner, and possession of loaded weapons in vehicles. Panther Warren Tucker wrote, "After we were arrested, booked, and fingerprinted, we were all put into the Drunk Tank, a large room with nothing in it but us. No bed, no blankets, nothing. This kind of treatment you expect from a racist dog. Then the beast called us out, one by one, to make a statement, but all the brothers told the racist dog to go to HELL. This is what I call Black UNITY."

After Huey learned that the Panthers had been arrested, he immediately began to raise bail money. He went to a local talk radio station where people were calling in wanting to hear more about what happened in Sacramento. Newton explained the Panthers' motivation for being in Sacramento, and the Party's agenda. Within twenty-four hours he had raised five thousand dollars. To amass such a sum so quickly, David Hilliard states that he and Huey invested five hundred dollars "in a pound of marijuana, breaking it down into nickels" and sold it.

Bobby Seale (30) and Mark Comfort (33) posted $2,200 bail that evening. Seven others were also held on $2,200 bail. Additional charges were placed against Eldridge Cleaver (31) for violation of parole; Reginald Forte (18) was charged with assault with a deadly weapon against a police officer. Most of the charges, except for conspiracy, were dropped. Those charged exclusively with conspiracy were Johnny Bethea (18), Ardell Butler (17), Kenneth Carter (19), Bruce Cockerhan (18), Albert Commo (21), Emory Douglas (23), George Dowell (28), James Dowell (17), Sherwin Forte (19), Truman Harris (18), Orleander Harrison, Jr. (17), Ernest Hatter (18), Mike Hall (18), Bobby Hutton (17), Lafayette Robinson (17), John Sloan (30), Willie Thompson (20), Lee Torris (22), Warren Tucker (19), Benny Yates (19).

Out on bail, the brothers were heroes in the community but identified as hoodlums in the white press. Seale did not want to go back to jail, so he decided to go underground. In Los Angeles he shaved his mustache, cut his hair, and wore sports clothes. His wife, Artie, barely recognized him when he picked her up at the bus station. Seale was determined to leave California, but he wanted to make sure that Artie and their son, Malik, were taken care of. Artie

Previous page: **A** state policeman escorts Panthers from the capitol in Sacramento on May 2, 1967.

Below: Panthers Bobby Seale, left, and Warren Tucker in the rear of the California State Assembly.

was under the impression that all of the Sacramento Panthers held on charges were going to get probation. The district attorney wanted Seale and six others to plead guilty to disturbing the Assembly. Seale's position was that he was not guilty, because the reporters led him astray onto the floor of the Assembly. Artie asked him, "Well, what's going to happen to everyone since you ain't going to show up?" Her question forced Bobby to rethink his position and the far-reaching impact of his actions. All the other brothers would go to jail for sure, and the ones on probation would really be in trouble. He then remembered Frantz Fanon's statement "We'd go to jail, those who are dedicated." Seale decided to go back to Oakland and do the time.

In the end, Sacramento officers were surprised when Cleaver asked permission in advance from his parole agent to take an assignment out of San Francisco. The law enforcement authorities were also peeved to learn that Cleaver's press credentials were legitimate and that his parole agent was aware of his activities. However, once he returned to San Francisco there were additional restrictions placed on his parole. Cleaver could not move beyond a designated seven-mile radius or cross the Bay Bridge. Clearly, this restriction resembled a slave code prohibiting his movement. Eldridge was to keep his name out of the newspapers for at least six months, he was not to make any more speeches, and he was not to write critically of the California Department of Corrections or any Californian politician. After two months, Cleaver's travel ban was lifted, but all other restrictions remained. Cleaver decided to lay low, but he continued to write for *Ramparts* magazine.

Sacramento led to the Black Panther Party's first national exposure. *US News and World Report* printed that California's capitol was the scene of demonstrations by armed Negroes identified as "Black Panthers." They reported the Panthers marched "armed with pistols, shotguns, and rifles" through the corridors crowded with schoolchildren. Governor Ronald Reagan said the incident was "a ridiculous way to solve problems that have to be solved among people of goodwill." The event was televised across the country and internationally. The Panthers' message was out.

The Sacramento event attracted new members, but the Panthers temporarily lost some rank-and-file members, and Chairman Seale. Seale and Warren Tucker were given the longest sentences, six months for "disturbing the peace." Though six months "was not long in the life" of their struggle, Huey was greatly saddened that Bobby would be gone, because he "was a good organizer, a man who got things moving." Thus began a series of arrests, bail, courts, and incarcerations for Panthers—a way to neutralize the organization slowly, by attrition. Seale was incarcerated in August 1967. Not until June 1971 were Huey and Bobby back on the streets together. Sacramento alarmed white America. For centuries African Americans had been ready to die for their liberation, but now they were armed, like Nat Turner in Virginia and Robert Williams in North Carolina, who defended their communities against vicious attacks. Panthers were prepared to pay the ultimate price of liberation with their own blood.

Left: **A**rmed Panther members stand in the capitol corridor to protest the bill before the Assembly that would restrict carrying loaded weapons in public.

Above top: They depart the capitol.

Above bottom: Panthers confront police officer before leaving the capitol.

OFFICE & NEWSPAPER

P anther Office No.1 had opened its doors in January 1967. It was located at 5624 Grove Street (now Martin Luther King, Jr., Way) in Oakland. Seale, Hutton, and Newton pooled their funds and rented a $150-per-month storefront. It was an ideal location in the heart of the North Oakland community, one block away from Merritt College. The majority of Merritt College students, like Seale and Newton, were Oakland residents who utilized the local college as a means to develop their intellectual and creative talents.

At the time the Party's office opened, Merritt College was experiencing a cultural renaissance. The campus became a magnet for philosophers, writers, playwrights, artists, and musicians. Bustling with students thirsty for knowledge and a newfound identity, every day the courtyard behind the main building served as a stage for fiery debates. The energy spilled over to the new Panther office.

Huey would challenge the armchair revolutionaries who really wanted to change conditions in the black community to join his ranks. That Newton was schooled in philosophical rhetoric made it difficult for his peers at Merritt College to dismiss his organization for not having a political base. Jerry Belcher, a staff writer for the *San Francisco Examiner*, went to the Party office in April 1967 and was captivated by Newton and Seale. He wrote, "Neither makes any bones about being revolutionary. 'We are a revolutionary party. The only solution for colonized people is revolutionary transition. Bloodshed is not necessary…but revolution often leads to it.'"

The office had a single desk, donated folding chairs, a long table, a chalkboard, and cheap red drapes cloaking the windows. Because the Panthers were without a mimeograph machine, Hutton and Seale, still employed at the Antipoverty Center, would make copies of the ten-point program at the center in the evenings.

Intellectual debates took place at official meetings on Wednesday nights at 7:00 P.M. and on Saturdays at 1:00 P.M. The police made it their business to step up surveillance of the Panther office during these time slots. Within the first couple of weeks, about twenty people would consistently attend the meetings. Some joined;

Previous page: **The tailor shop in Berkeley before it became the national Panther headquarters.**

Above: **A group of delegates to the national conference in front of the Black Panther National Headquarters in Berkeley, July 19, 1969.**

Right: **Bobby Hutton in front of the Oakland Police Department.**

others were supporters. The office soon became a place where community citizens could have their grievances addressed. Few children were allowed in the office because of the guns.

Police harassment and unjustified arrests were still major concerns. On May 22, 1967, three Oakland police officers were caught demolishing a neighborhood home without a search warrant. Word was out in the community that the Panthers would deal with any police officer who unjustly harassed anyone. After a young man ran to the Panther office and told Huey what was happening, Huey went to the house and ordered the officers to leave. He was arrested. When Bobby Seale went to bail Huey out of jail, he was arrested under an 1887 law barring possession of a gun near a jail.

As the Panthers continued to confront police, harassment within the community decreased; however, against the Panthers themselves it increased. One night in early June 1967, the Panthers attended a fundraising party in Richmond. No police had been in sight before the Panthers arrived. Because the officers stayed outside, the Panthers ignored their presence. At about 5:00 A.M. when the Panthers left the party, the cops were still parked outside. One

Panther, John Sloane, made a legal U turn, but the police directed him to the curb. The Panthers got into their patrol mode, despite the fact that they were unarmed. From a reasonable distance, they watched the officer's engagement with Sloan, who refused to sign the ticket, even though Huey had taught them to sign tickets and fight the police in court. By the time Huey walked over, at least eight police cars appeared on the scene. A cop began to club one of the Panthers. After Huey intervened, a scuffle broke out. Huey, Sloane, and the brother who was beaten were arrested. When they arrived at the police station, the cops worked them over until they were subdued. Huey was eventually charged with interfering with an arrest.

Despite the ongoing arrests and rotating periods of incarceration, the Panthers kept their office open. In Oakland alone between 1967 and 1973, they opened ten offices. During the peak year of 1968, five offices at different locations were available to the community.

Paying rent was always a challenge. With the assistance of Eldridge Cleaver, the Party began to produce pamphlets about the organization and "messages" from Newton and Cleaver. The sale of pamphlets, posters, buttons, and other memorabilia trickled in some funds. The money Panthers earned from their outside employment or lectures was also used to keep the Party going. But in the end, money from the sale of *The Black Panther: Black Community News*

Left: **P**anther members Bobby Hutton and Reginald Forte at the Oakland Police Department, May 1967.

Below: **Bobby Hutton, right, and Bobby Seale, at the Oakland Police Department.**

Service, the Party's newspaper, generated a steady cash flow. The newspaper sold for twenty-five cents; it cost ten cents to produce and distribute, and the Panthers, none of whom received a salary from the Party, earned ten cents from every newspaper they sold. The newspaper offered the youth in the community an avenue to earn money. The Party earned five cents off every newspaper sold. Several black businesses placed ads in early editions.

Just as the Black Panther office was the location where citizens could air their grievances, so *The Black Panther* became the community's medium to write about various issues and share solutions.

Denzil Dowell's wanton murder had made the Panthers realize they needed their own newspaper to explain to the community what really happened. Despite the fact there were only six full-time Panthers, the community mobilized to produce the first issue of *The Black Panther* on April 25, 1967, devoted exclusively to Dowell's murder. The four-page newspaper substantiated its story with the coroner's report that stipulated that Dowell's arms were raised above his head at the time he was shot. In addition, *The Black Panther* presented interviews with family members who detailed the harassment they experienced after the killing because of their unwillingness to be silent about the murder.

The second issue of *The Black Panther* was also devoted to one single story, "The Truth About Sacramento." The opening began, "May 2, 1967—we will quickly run it down, since the mass media has indulged itself in an orgy of distortion, lying, and misrepresentations seldom equaled in the history of racist U.S.A."

The May 15, 1967 issue included a strong message to law enforcement agencies about their duties as officers and the rights of the people they are paid to serve. "TO COPS: We are here to civilize you. We are here to teach you how to love and serve the people with a humble and faithful attitude consistent with your status. We are going to do the job whether you like it or not." Clearly, the Panthers utilized their newspaper as a means to counterattack mainstream press analysis of events that had a direct impact on the black community.

There were other radical newspapers—*The Flatlands, Oakland Post, Berkeley Barb,* and *Muhammad Speaks*, but *The Black Panther* was different, because it taught courage, gave black people practical legal advice on how to survive in racist America, and represented the voices of the "brother and sister on the block." At the height of repression, only *The Black Panther* became a vehicle for the prisoners to communicate with their families, lawyers, and community. Important court dates, events schedules, outcomes of trials were listed. *The Black Panther* also exposed how the white press misrepresented African Americans by relying on negative stereotypes. Cleaver served as the first editor of the newspaper, and David DuBois, son of W.E.B. DuBois, was one of its last.

Production of the early Party newspapers was all done by hand. In the mid-1960s the Panthers had only T-square rulers, scissors, matte knives, screens, pressdown type, drawing boards, a few typewriters, and border tapes. The staff consisted of contributing writers, editors, and photographers. Yet one of the most noteworthy features of the Panther newspaper was the visuals.

Publishing and distributing was a full-time project for many of the Black Panthers.

THE BLACK PANTHER

25 cents

Black Community News Service

VOLUME 1	MAY 15, 1967	NUMBER 2

PUBLISHED WEEKLY BY **THE BLACK PANTHER PARTY FOR SELF DEFENSE** P. O. Box 8641 Emmeryville Br. Oakland, Calif.

The Truth About SACRAMENTO

THESE ARE THREE OF THE TWENTY-THREE COURAGEOUS BROTHERS AT THE CAPITOL. THEY ARE REPRESENTATIVES OF THE SPIRIT OF 67. "IS RIGHTEOUSLY ARMED AND READY FOR ACTION."

To get a clear picture of the significance of Black Panther day - May 2, 1967 -we will quickly run it down, since the mass media has indulged itself in an orgy of distortion, lying, and misrepresentation seldom equaled in the history of racist U.S.A. Uniformly, the mass media has refused to report the chain of events that led up to the visit of the Black Panthers to the capitol.

April 1, 1967, Denzil Dowell, age 22, was killed by a racist cop on the Contra Costa Sheriff's Department force. The press has repeatedly failed to incorporate the outrage experienced in the black community with the subsequent actions of the Black Panther Party. The facts of Denzil's murder, as prepared by the Dowell's attorney, are as follows: 1) The doctor on the case told the relatives that Denzil must have been shot with his hands raised. 2) The cornor's report stated there were 6 bullet holes, while the newspapers called the Richmond Independent said there were only 3 bullet holes. White America appears content as a whole to buy the Three Bullet Theory in the Kennedy murder, but black people will not buy the Three Bullet Theory in the Denzil Dowell murder. 3) The Cornor said that death was due to bleeding, yet

no blood was found at the site of the body. The Dowell family was denied the right to take pictures of the body, or to this day both the Richmond police and Martinez police have refused to return Denzil's clothes for further necessary evidence pertinent to the findings. No clearer case of unjustifiable homicide exists. No entry had been made into the building that the killer-cop assumed Denzil had robbed. Denzil had a hip injury which the cop was aware of, as he had arrested him before. Denzil did not have a gun, and this could have been detected by a trained protector of society. So how could 6 bullets have ever been justifiable?
(continued on page 5)

TO BLOODS

If any cop brutalizes you or violates your Human Rights, beats you, threatens you, or tries to intimidate you, please, please, please, get his picture or his name if he is civilized enough to give it to you; or get his badge number. As soon as you get all this information, turn it over to the Black Panther Party for Self Defense and the Party will deal with it in an appropriate manner.

TO COPS

We don't like the way you cops have been misusing the law and mistreating the people. You are civil servants, which means that the people - all the people - have delegated to you the task of securing the people in the daily exercise of their rights. For example: the function of removing waste material from our commodes was delegated by the people to those we call
(continued on page 2)

FOREFRONT, TREASURER AND CHAIRMAN BOBBY SEALE OF B.P.P.S.D.

Statement BY MINISTER OF DEFENSE TO THE BLACK WORLD

Below is the statement prepared by Huey P. Newton, Minister of Defense, and delivered by Bobby Seale, Chairman, of the Black Panther Party for Self-Defense, May 2, 1967, at the state capitol in Sacramento, California. When this statement is read carefully, it becomes obvious that all that is here is TRUTH. Knowing full well they were legally exercising their constitutional rights, the Panthers made fools of the cops who tried to take the guns away from them, and suffered the humiliation of having to give them right back. The dumb Capitol cops didn't even know their own gun laws. Continued on page 2

THE WHITE COMMUNITY

TO RACIST SHERIFF YOUNGER DENZIL DOWELL IS JUST ANOTHER DEAD NIGGER.

THE BLACK COMMUNITY

SUPPORT YOUR LOCAL POLICE

Emory Douglas was the Party's minister of culture. His artwork set the visual tone for *The Black Panther* and became the model for revolutionary art in the 1960s. His explosive illustrations captured the attention of readers and offered them the "correct picture of the struggle whereas the Revolutionary Ideology gives the people the correct political understanding of our struggle." Douglas's work represented black people as powerful, dignified, passionate freedom fighters. The key to liberation art was to "feel what the people feel who throw rocks and bottles at the oppressor so that when we draw about it…we can raise their level of consciousness to hand grenades and dynamite to be launched at the oppressor."

Emory's drawings of the oppressor as weak, low-life, mindless pigs are just as legendary. When Huey decided to put a pig in the newspaper with the badge number of an officer who had a history of harassing folks, Emory responded, "My man, why don't we dress them up, like humans, and stand them up?" And that's what he did. He unmasked the oppressor in a fashion that allowed black people to "cut through the smoke screens" created by their exploiters and empower themselves for action. One can imagine overthrowing swine easier than an institution. Emory's visual representations were humorous and heart-wrenching. He captured the spirit of the people's willingness to struggle for liberation at all costs.

Everyone had access to Emory's art. Unlike artists who displayed their works in museums and galleries or sold their work to the highest bidder, Emory's work graced the walls outside city buildings, telephone poles, and Panther households.

The powerful artwork of Emory and his assistant, Matilaba, even caught the eye of the FBI. When police officers riddled the Panther office with bullets, they were sure to target the posters and other artwork. COINTELPRO (FBI counterintelligence program) took notice of the impact that Party artwork had on the people in the community. It was reproduced for international publications and exhibited in Africa, Asia, and Latin America.

Emory re-created so many Panther activities and intense moments of crisis because he was there. When the Panthers went to Sacramento, Emory was present; Emory was at "Free Huey" rallies; Emory assisted in the layout and production of *The Black Panther*. His commitment to the black struggle and his implementation of art as a tool for liberation are unsurpassed.

The articles in *The Black Panther* were concise, and the political position of the organization was not camouflaged with empty rhetoric. The Panthers attacked obvious enemies, such as the police, but they also exposed popular black leaders in their "bootlickers gallery"—local black politicians, as well as national leaders such as Bayard Rustin, Martin Luther King, Jr., and Roy Wilkins. The newspaper also ran eyewitness accounts, photographs, and written statements from victims of police brutality throughout the country. It chronicled blacks in the military, inferior education, prison conditions, along with international news.

By March 16, 1969, *The Black Panther* was sold at twenty-six locations throughout the United States. In 1969-70 they printed over 105,000 copies per week. The Los Angeles Panthers sold 6,000

copies in three days. This was considered high-volume circulation for underground newspapers.

It took all the Bay Area Panthers to produce and distribute *The Black Panther*. Eventually the Wednesday night meetings were transferred to the Fulton district in San Francisco. All available comrades went to San Francisco to prepare the newspaper for distribution. A former Panther, Assata, wrote in her memoir how they worked until the early morning sorting, labeling, and bundling the newspaper to be shipped across the country. They sang songs and Panther marching chants. The community continued to support the Panthers—from high school students to elderly men and women.

Bobby Seale details the difficulty they had publishing and distributing *The Black Panther*. First, the Party received a letter from the printers union explaining that since their paper was of "professional quality," its producers had to be union members. Several key members of the newspaper committee joined the union. In May 1969, Howard Quinn Printing Company in San Francisco received bomb threats for printing the paper. Other times newspapers would arrive at their destinations wet, late, and unreadable. Still others were confiscated by the FBI or deliberately sent to the wrong destination. The Party was forced to send the newspapers COD because the airlines too often held up shipping.

David Hilliard wrote about the power of *The Black Panther* not only "to inform but to organize. If the brother takes the copy, I've made a potential convert."

SUPPORT YOUR LOCAL POLICE

FREE HUEY

By the end of May 1967, the Party began receiving requests to start branches outside of Oakland. Huey knew that the organization needed an administrative core to expand effectively. He hoped that members of the Student Nonviolent Coordinating Committee (SNCC), highly skilled and disciplined workers, could assist the Panthers. Perhaps the two could merge, since the momentum of the civil rights movement in the South was on the wane. Eldridge, Bobby, and Huey planned to draft SNCC leaders Stokely Carmichael as Panther prime minister, H. Rap Brown as minister of justice, and James Forman as minister of foreign affairs. The merger never materialized because of miscommunication and basic lack of trust. However, Huey did issue Executive Mandate No. 2, which officially inducted Stokely Carmichael as the Black Panther field marshal.

The Panthers continued to patrol against police violence. By June 1967 they added traffic control to their agenda. Over two years, three children had been killed and seven injured coming from school at the intersection of 55th and Market streets in Oakland. Huey and Bobby heard many complaints from community members about the dire need to do something. Together they suggested to the Antipoverty Advisory Committee that a petition be sent to the Office of Economic Opportunity Community Complaints (EOCC) requesting a traffic signal. While the Panthers collected all the signatures for the petition, Huey had the opportunity to meet the children who crossed at the intersection. They were calling themselves Black Panthers, but their goal was to fight other kids. The children were simply mimicking the white media's representation of the Panthers.

Huey and other Panthers decided to organize the children into Junior Panthers. The Panthers explained the goals of the Party and told the pupils not to hate white people but to learn to love themselves and work with others. The Junior Panthers were between the ages of twelve and fourteen, and an intermediate group ranged from eight to twelve. They were taught black history and the application of revolutionary ideas. Children were not allowed in the Panther office because of its guns, so Huey used the Antipoverty Center to teach the class.

The Oakland City Council responded to the Panther petitions that it would take more than a year to place a signal light at the intersection. Huey retorted that an officer should be placed at the intersection to direct traffic during peak periods. If the city refused to address this demand, the Panthers would direct traffic, armed with their guns, to save the lives of black children. True to their word, they worked as crossing guards, directing traffic when necessary. The Panthers' unwillingness to wait passively for action forced the Oakland City Council to change its tune and make the intersection a priority. On August 1, 1967, work for the signal light began.

During the summer of 1967, rebellions once again fanned throughout urban America. Insurrections in Cleveland, Detroit, and Newark were linked to economic despair and police violence. Black Power advocates' cultural revolution offered a renewed sense of black consciousness that influenced school curricula with cultural awareness programs in the arts, fashion, language, and hairstyles. But it was not enough to quell African Americans' justified anger and frustration. The Panthers broadened the Black Power call with the slogan "All Power to the People." The inhabitants of particular communities should be in the position to control the institutions that shape their livelihood. Black unity would serve as the catalyst to revolutionize humanity.

Below: **Children demonstrating outside the courthouse where Huey was on trial.**

Americans were also enraged by the Vietnam War. Free speech proponents, some of whom were hippies, led this charge of civil disobedience. The Oakland Induction Center was a major site for mass demonstrations in the Bay Area. Many white observers were outraged by the chemical Mace and clubs used by the Oakland police department to quash the picket lines and sit-ins, despite their common use in the black community.

Without a doubt, black citizens needed protection from the police. When the Mulford Act passed the California legislative body and was signed into law in August 1967, the Panther patrols with loaded guns were technically illegal. They no longer could protect themselves against arbitrary police barbarity. To carry an unloaded gun was suicidal. The display of guns made the Panthers easy targets of the police, but Newton believed they had proved the point that black people had to arm themselves against their oppressor. If black people had a basic knowledge of their constitutional rights, many confrontations with officers that often escalated into arrests, fisticuffs, and murder could be avoided. To empower the people, Newton wrote the "Pocket Lawyer of Legal First Aid." The fourteen rules, instructing citizens how to handle police officers, were listed in *The Black Panther* regularly, beginning with the May 15, 1967, edition.

The Oakland community read the Party's newspaper and took the Party's advice. Committed Panthers had trickled into the organization, but the Party was still the brainchild of Huey P. Newton and Bobby Seale. In early May 1967, Eldridge Cleaver staged the scene of Huey's famous wicker chair poster. Bobby wrote that the shields in the picture "represented a shield for black people against all the imperialism, the decadence, the aggression, and the racism in this country." Huey did not really like the symbolic nature of the poster but sat for the photo.

When Huey was not working, he would spend twelve to fourteen hours a day talking to whomever would listen about the Black Panther Party. He went not only to Merritt College, but also to bars, pool halls, and parks—wherever black folks assembled. Even high school students from Oakland Technical High, McClymonds, and Castlemont heard Huey's message via Black Student Union meetings and *The Black Panther*. Huey reflected, "It was work that had profound significance for me; the very meaning of my life was in it, and it brought me closer to the people."

On October 27, Huey celebrated his last day of probation for the assault of Odell Lee. He began his day by speaking at "The Future of the Black Liberation Movement," hosted by the BSU of San Francisco State College. Newton did not like speaking to crowds, but with Bobby Seale in jail he had to pick up the slack. The students were politically astute and challenged Huey on the Panthers' readiness to work with white activists. Many black students were suspicious of whites, a viewpoint Huey understood. But he felt it failed to take into consideration the limitations of black power. He argued that as long as the Panthers controlled the programs, coalitions with young white activists were "worth the risk." During this period the Party was the only cutting-edge black organization willing to work with nonblack allies.

POCKET LAWYER OF LEGAL FIRST AID

This pocket lawyer is provided as a means of keeping black people up to date on their rights. We are always the first to be arrested and the racist police forces are constantly trying to pretend that rights are extended equally to all people. Cut this out, brothers and sisters, and carry it with you. Until we arm ourselves to righteously take care of our own, the pocket lawyer is what's happening.

1. If you are stopped and/or arrested by the police, you may remain silent; you do not have to answer any questions about alleged crimes, you should provide your name and address only if requested (although it is not absolutely clear that you must do so). But then do so, and at all times remember the fifth amendment.
2. If a police officer is not in uniform, ask him to show his identification. He has no authority over you unless he properly identifies himself. Beware of persons posing as police officers. Always get his badge number and his name. . . .
8. As soon as you have been booked, you have the right to complete at least two phone calls—one to a relative, friend or attorney, the other to a bail bondsman. If you can, call the Black Panther Party, 654-2003, and the Party will post bail if possible....
13. If you do not have the money to hire an attorney, immediately ask the police to get you an attorney without charge....

That evening Huey had dinner with his family and then proceeded to his local hangout, Bosn's Locker. After he left this bar, he went to a couple of parties, and finally met his longtime friend Gene McKinney. Together they went to another social gathering in Oakland, and left at about 4:00 A.M. As Huey drove the car down Seventh Street, he was pulled over by Police Officer John Frey, who knew he had a Panther car because of the "hot sheet" that listed autos owned by Party members. Frey radioed into the station at 4:56 A.M., "It's a known Black Panther vehicle . . . you might send a unit by." The dispatcher, Officer Clarence Lord, sent out backup Officer Herbert Heanes. Frey had a notorious reputation in Oakland as one of the worst "pigs." Huey knew the routine: he was ordered out of the car and complied. Huey picked up his law book (his name was written inside the flyleaf) to read the law to the "law enforcer." Gene McKinney remembered Officer Frey saying, "Well, we got the great Huey P. Newton." It "dawns" on McKinney that "they're trying to kill us—trying to kill Huey." Newton recalled that Officer Frey "snarled, 'You can take that book and shove it up your ass, nigger.'" Frey then hit Newton, who fell to the ground. As Huey "started to rise, I saw the officer draw his service revolver, point it at me, and fire." Officer Heanes testified to the grand jury that at no time did he see a gun in Huey's hand. However, a barrage of shots came from somewhere, because Frey was killed and Heanes wounded. Gene got out of the car and saw "Huey and one cop entangled; the other cop is shooting." McKinney pulled Newton away from the scene, unbeknownst to him leaving Huey's California criminal law book a few feet away from Officer Frey. Gene hailed a friend of his in a car, who drove them to David Hilliard's house.

Hilliard saw the pain Huey was in and insisted they take Newton to the hospital. Huey responded, "If you take me to the hospital, all they're gonna do is kill me . . . And if I go to jail, I'll go to the gas chamber." David and his brother June took an unconscious Huey to Kaiser Hospital at 5:40 A.M., and then went to Eldridge Cleaver's home in San Francisco. After hearing what had happened, Eldridge asked about Huey's clothes. "We gotta get rid of them." Cleaver is "already thinking about the trial." David and June returned to Oakland. David remembered all of Cleaver's instructions: He burned the clothes, organized the Party to deal effectively with the press, and kept in close contact with Huey's family. Cleaver granted Hilliard the title of captain of the national headquarters. Hilliard was relieved he had passed Cleaver's "initiation" test: "I've become a member of the Party; the problems of my life—my restlessness, my sense of purposelessness—are resolved."

At Kaiser Hospital the medical attendants refused Huey treatment, ignoring the four bullets in his abdomen and one in his thigh. The manhunt for Huey was intense. It took the Oakland police department only thirteen minutes to arrive at the shooting scene and target Newton as the prime suspect.

Officer Lord dispatched: Additional information on Huey Newton. He's a light-skinned Negro and he has his hair piled up pretty high on his head.

Another officer: It's real fuzzy and soft, but not piled up high. Just a lot of hair.

Opposite: **T**he famous poster of Huey Newton, minister of defense of the Black Panther Party.

Officer Lord: Check. It's one of those fuzzy-hairdos. The latest style.

Another officer: No grease.

Officer Lord: Check, original style hair.

Officer: African style. . .

Officers handcuffed Newton to both sides of the gurney. The police hit Newton from his handcuffed wrists to his bloody stomach. The officers exclaimed, "You're going to die for this. . . . If you don't die in the gas chamber, then when you're sent to prison we'll have you killed there, and if you're acquitted we'll kill you in the streets." When they spat at him, Huey mustered enough strength and "spat blood in their faces and over their uniforms. Finally, the doctor put a towel over my mouth, and the police continued their attacks." Officers pointed guns at his head and threatened to cut his intravenous tubes. Newton was then moved to Highland-Alameda County Hospital, because he "was not a member of the Kaiser health plan."

The October 28, 1967, *Oakland Tribune* headline exclaimed, "Officer Slain in Gun Battle." Newton's photo was on the front page as he lay handcuffed to a gurney. As word spread throughout the community, Huey's health and welfare became a major concern. Matilaba recalled that the parking lot of Highland Hospital was filled with Panthers and community supporters. The Oakland police came out in full force and attitude to secure their infamous prisoner. Newton was eventually moved to the Alameda County jail and charged with kidnapping, murder, and attempted murder. The Party scrambled to assemble a legal team to keep Huey out of the gas chamber. The selection of a black or a white lawyer became a central issue. The Panthers wanted to keep Newton alive. They selected Charles R. Garry, a white attorney, who had a personal commitment to equal justice under the law and a record of defending more than thirty capital cases; none of the defendants in these received the gas chamber. The Panthers suggested to disgruntled black lawyers that they form a committee to work on other pending cases.

Many Panthers agreed that Cleaver was the most effective public speaker in the Party with Seale and Newton incarcerated. Cleaver was a master of words, both written and spoken. Once he got the nuns in a convent to join him in a chant, "Fuck Ronald Reagan." After much coaxing from Eldridge, the nuns repeated the slogan. Cleaver concluded, "Now, you're liberated in speech." He repeated his "Fuck Ronald Reagan" chant at Stanford University and wherever he felt like saying it.

Eldridge had the ability to articulate political currents with ease; he dazzled white America and made black America proud. Cleaver's writings about Newton removed the gun-toting-thug image perpetuated by the media. He conveyed the message that Huey was the heart and soul of the Party, a political leader whose presence could not be denied. By November, Eldridge and his wife, Kathleen, began making speeches on Huey's defense and writing articles criticizing the police and politicians. In Cleaver's zeal to keep Newton out of the gas chamber, he broke all restrictions placed upon him by his parole agents and capitalized on all visual and written forms of

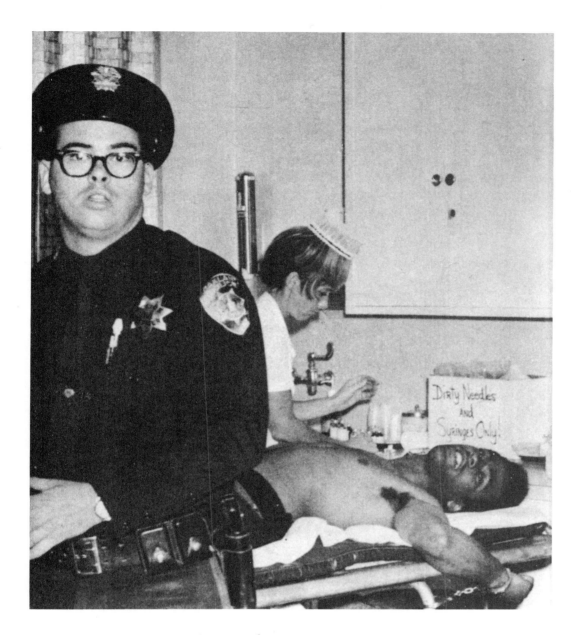

communication. On December 8, 1967, Bobby Seale was released from jail; thus, Cleaver cut back drastically on his public activities, hoping the parole board would back off him. Behind the scenes, Cleaver strategically searched for nonblack allies. At this point Seale took the lead in the "Free Huey" campaign.

"Black is beautiful, free Huey; set our warrior free, off the pig" were the cries of the Black Panthers. Seale spoke at college campuses and rallies. Panthers walked the streets selling newspapers and asking for donations for Huey's defense. Activists from various BSUs and other black organizations and churches assisted the Panthers in developing an elaborate campaign with publicity, finance, and legal committees. Sympathetic whites formed "Honkies for Huey." Under the guidance of Erica McClain, white radicals published leaflets announcing Huey's political agenda and trial dates, and organized fund raisers. Some activists in Ann Arbor, Michigan formed a White Panther Party. The Oakland police department

Above: **H**uey, wounded and manacled to a gurney, in the emergency room of Kaiser Hospital after the Sergeant Frey shoot-out.

Above: **C**harles Garry (right) and Huey Newton.

Opposite left: **Eldridge Cleaver and Chico Neblett.**

Opposite right: **Kathleen Cleaver.**

continued its assault on the Panthers. They arrested Hilliard on January 15, 1968, while he was passing out Party leaflets at Oakland Technical High School. The following day at 3:30 A.M. San Francisco police officers busted down the Cleavers' apartment door, and drew guns on Kathleen, Eldridge, and Emory, then searched and ransacked the apartment without a search warrant.

The Panthers pressed onward and organized a major "Free Huey" rally on his birthday, February 17. It was held across the street from the Alameda County Courthouse, where Huey was jailed. More than five thousand supporters attended. Eldridge was the master of ceremonies. Other speakers included Stokely Carmichael (prime minister), who refused to wear a Panther uniform and opted for African garb; H. Rap Brown (minister of justice); and James Forman (minister of foreign affairs). Bunchy Carter was introduced as the minister of defense for southern California. Representatives of the Peace and Freedom Party, at the behest of Eldridge Cleaver, were also present. More than ten thousand dollars was raised. The next day the Southern California chapter held a "Free Huey" rally. Bunchy Carter and Earl Anthony worked with Ron Karenga's United Slaves (US) organization, the best-organized black nationalist group in Los Angeles. This was the first and last occasion that Panthers and US members were comrades in the liberation struggle.

As the Panthers intensified their commitment to defend Huey, the Bay Area police kept pace to destroy the organization. On February 25, 1968, at 3:00 A.M. Bobby and Artie Seale were arrested at their home in Berkeley. Though the Seales and policemen provided conflicting stories on what actually occurred, they both agreed that Bobby yelled, "Don't kill my wife! Don't kill my wife!" The Panthers understood that their lives were in jeopardy when left alone with officers. Bobby was charged with "conspiracy to commit murder." Their bond was $11,000. Charges were later dropped for lack of evidence. The same night Bunchy Carter (25), Anthony Coltrale (28), Audre Hudson (31), and David Hilliard (25) were arrested and charged with carrying concealed weapons. The Party held a press conference and demonstration the following day damning the arrests, blatant harassment, and attempts to drain funds from the organization. By the end of the month, twenty-four additional Oakland Panthers were arrested, with charges ranging from profanity to inciting a riot. There were also mass arrests in Nashville and a massive shooting in Orangeburg, South Carolina. H. Rap Brown was arrested immediately following his appearance at the "Free Huey" rally. Huey reacted from jail by issuing Executive Mandate No. 3.

". . . We will not fall victim to a St. Valentine's Massacre. Therefore, those who approach our doors in the manner of outlaws, who seek to enter our homes illegally, unlawfully, and in a rowdy fashion, those who kick our doors down with no authority, who seek to ransack our homes in violation of our human rights will henceforth be treated as outlaws, as gangsters, as evildoers. We have no way of determining that a man in a uniform involved in a forced outlaw entry into our homes is in fact a guardian of the law. He is acting like a lawbreaker and we must make the appropriate response. We draw the line at the threshold of our doors."

LEROY ELDRIDGE CLEAVER was born in 1935 in Wabbaseka, a small town near Pine Bluff, Arkansas. His father Leroy was a pianist and waiter, while his mother Thelma taught elementary school. Soon after the family moved to Watts in Los Angeles, his parents separated, and Eldridge stayed with his mother. She was forced to work as a janitress at a junior high school in Los Angeles. In junior high, Eldridge experienced his first arrest, when he was accused of petty theft and sentenced to a boys reformatory. Upon his release, he was an astute hustler.

By this time his mother had moved to South Pasadena. Eldridge enrolled at Belmont High School and prior to graduation was caught with a shopping bag full of marijuana. Once again he was sent to a reformatory school—the notorious Preston School of Industry. On June 18, 1954, after his eighteenth birthday, he was sent to Soledad Prison to serve the remainder of his sentence.

Cleaver writes, "In Soledad state prison, I fell in with a group of young blacks, who, like myself, were in vociferous rebellion against what we perceived as a continuation of slavery on a higher plane." While in prison he became a voracious reader and completed the course work for his high school diploma. Yet Eldridge's most disturbing change was his ambivalent attitude toward white women. He was released from Soledad in late 1956 and was incarcerated again by late 1957. He was charged with assault and intent to kill and given a two-to-fourteen-year sentence. Cleaver writes in *Soul on Ice* that while in Soledad he "became a rapist." On parole he "crossed the tracks and sought out white prey. I did this consciously, deliberately, willfully, methodically—though looking back I see that I was in a frantic, wild, and completely abandoned frame of mind." After his return to prison, he admitted he was wrong and that he had gone "astray—astray not so much from the white man's law as from being human, civilized—for I could not approve the act of rape."

Eldridge underwent a profound change at both San Quentin and Folsom Prisons. He became a follower of Malcolm X and a minister for the Nation of Islam. After Malcolm was ostracized from the Nation, Eldridge also cut his ties with the Nation. He "ran a regular public campaign for Malcolm in Folsom. I saw to it that copies of his speeches were circulated among Negro inmates." In Cleaver's efforts to give legal support for black prisoners' religious freedoms, he wrote attorneys. Attorney Beverly Axelrod received a letter, visited him in Folsom, and ultimately orchestrated his release on December 13, 1966. Eldridge's parole was designated a "Special Study Case" and he was required to see his parole agent four times a month. Eldridge wrote that from his "16th year, I spent the next 15 in and out of prison, the last time being an unbroken stay of 9 years."

Eldridge gave some of his writings to Beverly, who submitted them to Ramparts Press in San Francisco. Attorney Edward Keaton promised to hire Eldridge as a writer upon his release. Keaton kept his word, and Eldridge left Los Angeles and took his parole to San Francisco. He edited and published his prison letters in February 1968. The book, *Soul on Ice*, became a best seller.

With Huey in jail, the Panthers organized to raise money for his defense and demonstrated for a new trial and his freedom.

The "Free Huey" campaign galvanized the Party. "Free Huey" bumper stickers and buttons appeared throughout the Bay Area. *The Black Panther* increased its circulation tenfold, and membership interest soared. Daily the new Party office, located at Forty-fifth and Grove Streets, received phone calls from all over the country inquiring about membership. The Panthers created a structure for new chapters: Individuals had to come to Oakland and sell *The Black Panther*, memorize the organization's rules and Party platform, and attend political education classes. Seale was adamant that this course be followed because he feared undisciplined brothers. Case in point: a Brooklyn chapter organized by an Oakland native, Ron Penniwell, who concentrated on citizen arrests of police who were drunk or asleep on duty. While arresting police was inventive, it was not the direction of the Party. Seale found himself trapezing from state to state clarifying the Party's program and rules, while raising money for Huey's defense. By April 1968 the Black Panther Party had chapters

HAPPY BIRTHDAY HUEY

Fund Raising Birthday Benefit for

HUEY P. NEWTON

BY THE NEWTON-CLEAVER DEFENSE COMMITTEE

Sunday, Feb. 16, Berkeley Community Theatre

BERKELEY HIGH SCHOOL AT **7:00 PM**
GROVE & ALLSTON WAY

Speakers:
KATHLEEN CLEAVER
TOM HAYDEN
ATTORNEY CHARLES GARRY
FATHER EARL NEIL
RAY "MAASI" HEWETT   LA BPP·

WITH:
LE BALLET AFRO-HAITI
Rev. George Johnson & guitar
films: "Off the Pigs" &
"Prelude to Revolution"
Baby Dee reading the poetry of
Alprentice "Bunchy" Carter
Johnny Talbot & De Thangs

東
FREE
HUEY

YELLOW
PERIL
SUPPORTS
BLACK
POWER

in Los Angeles, New York, Chicago, and Seattle.

There was no typical Panther, nor a standard day in the life of a full-time, dedicated, loyal Party member. Though Panther experiences in Oakland may have differed from those in other cities, they all pledged to serve as revolutionary freedom fighters for their communities by implementing the Party's ten-point program.

The majority of Panthers were male and between the ages of sixteen and twenty-five. The Party initially directed its membership call to men because of its self-defense emphasis. The concluding statement on the first issue of *The Black Panther*, April 25, 1967, was a summons to men:

Black Panther members outside the Alameda County Court house protesting Huey Newton's trial.

BLACK MEN!!!: It is your duty to your women and children, to your mothers and sisters, to investigate the program of the PARTY. There is no other way. We have tried everything else. This is the moment in history when Black people have no choice but to move and move rapidly to gain their freedom, justice and all the other ingredients of civilized living that have been denied to us. This is where it is at. Check it out, Black Brothers and Sisters. This is our DAY!!!!!

However, women such as Artie Seale, LaVerne Williams, Matilaba, Betty Carter, Sandra Gipson, JoAnn Mitchell, Patricia Hilliard, Janis Forte, Betty Bogard, Gail Bell, Ora Sanders, and Kathleen Cleaver were loyal members during the early days. Though few in number, these women participated, contributed, and sacrificed just like the men in the organization. In fact, during the early period women and men were liberated from gender-specific duties. As the Party proliferated during the "Free Huey" campaign, female membership profoundly increased.

The first step for Party membership was to fill out a form and donate three dollars to the organization "if you had it" or fifty cents "if you did not." During the early days of recruitment, very few people were turned down. One was required to participate in a six-week program that included political education (PE) classes divided into three parts: community, leadership, and cadre. The National Headquarters (Oakland) created a standard format, under the direction of George Murray, minister of education, and sent weekly lessons to chapters. They read books such as Franz Fanon's *Wretched of the Earth*, Mao's *Red Book*, *The Autobiography of Malcolm X*, and Kwame Nkrumah's *I Speak of Freedom*. For most members this was their first opportunity to learn historical truths about African and American history. Many Panthers argued that the Party book list contained the first relevant material

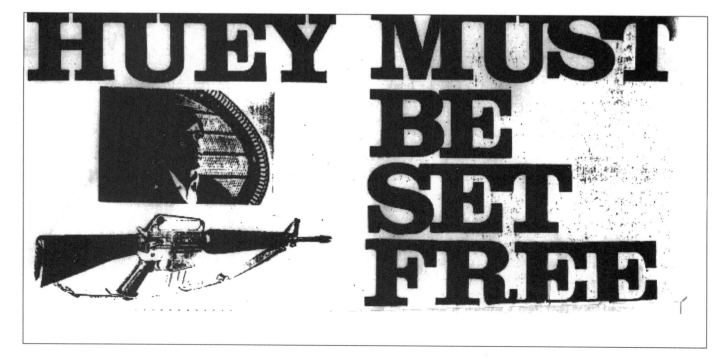

they ever read. During this initiation process they also read and discussed material in local newspapers and *The Black Panther*. They had to memorize the ten-point program and Party rules.

New recruits were also encouraged to write essays, reports, and poetry, and contribute to the Party's newspaper. This regimen automatically developed reading and writing skills. Some members watched the eventually banned movie, *The Battle of Algiers*, a film that detailed how the Algerian people expelled the French from Algeria. Recruits also learned the duties of the Panther positions. Captains were the highest-ranking officers of the rank-and-file membership. They linked the ministries and footsoldiers; they negotiated on behalf of both groups. New recruits had to take a pass/fail test.

The new recruits were then sectioned into cadres (five to six members), which in many ways functioned like extended families. Cadres studied and worked together and watched each other's backs. Many cadres would eventually live together in the same apartment or house. Some of the volunteer duties that Panthers performed included cleaning up, security, officer of the day, secretarial, distribution and sale of newspapers, cooking, answering phones, enlisting donations, distributing leaflets, announcing community activities, posting leaflets and posters, transportation, sales of buttons and posters.

Above: In front from left, Ben Stewart, head of San Francisco State Black Student Union; George Murray, teacher suspended from San Francisco State; and Bobby Seale.

Below: A march in New York City in support of Huey.

Opposite: **P**anthers Catherine Perry, foreground, and Sheila Roach, left, after arrest following police raid on what police called the New Bedford, Mass. Black Panther headquarters.

Below: Black Panthers demonstrating.

The final stage of the initiation process was technical and military training. Panthers were taught respect for weapons, how to clean and assemble artillery. Some Panthers had secret membership and concealed their affiliation for personal employment purposes. After spending six weeks in the initiation program, Panthers were armed with information about why they were oppressed and had the courage to change their conditions.

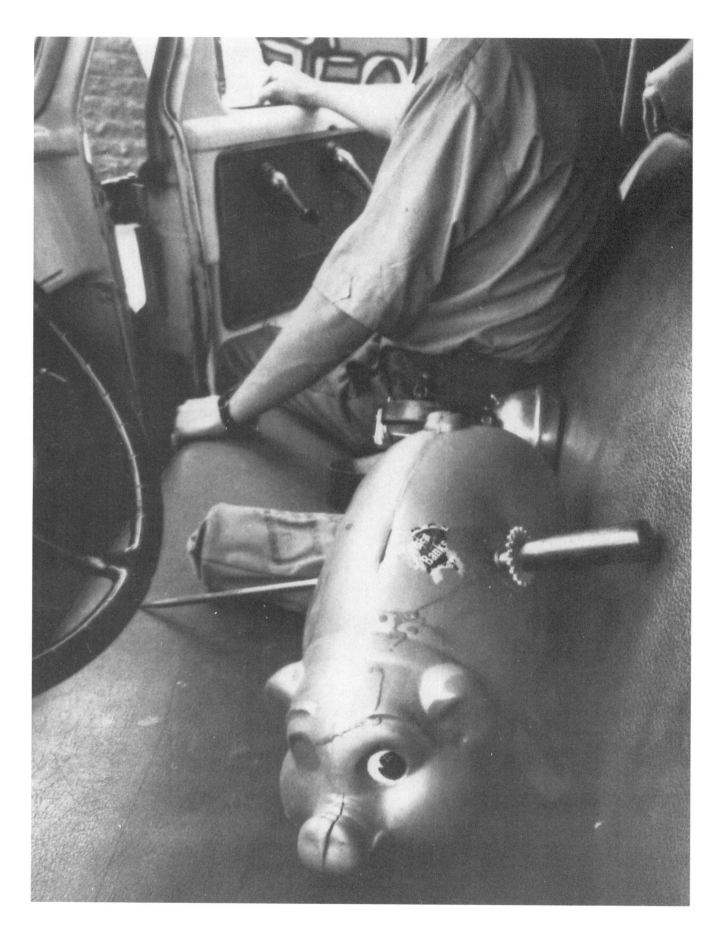

POLICE ACTIVITY

As membership in the Black Panther Party spanned the United States, local police departments stepped up their unwarranted violent attacks against Party members. In August 1967, the Federal Bureau of Investigation (FBI) began lurking around Party members. On March 4, 1968, it plunged into the Panther mix. J. Edgar Hoover issued a memorandum outlining goals to his staff. "1. Prevent the coalition of militant black nationalist groups. In unity there is strength . . . black nationalist groups might be the first step toward a real Mau Mau [militant group in Kenya organized in 1951 to fight white colonial rule]. 2. Prevent the rise of a black Messiah who would unify and electrify the black nationalist movement."

The FBI was founded in July 1908 as the U.S. government's political police force, and J. Edgar Hoover was hired as the FBI's sixth director in 1924. For the next forty-eight years, until his death May 2, 1972, Hoover ran the FBI as a dictatorship. With vengeance, he attacked individuals and organizations whom he perceived to be a threat to U.S. security. When no real threat existed, he manufactured one. Hoover used illegal tactics and murder when all else failed.

During March 1968, Arthur (Glen) Morris, brother of Bunchy Carter, was shot by "agents of the U.S. government." He was the first member of the Black Panther Party killed. That same month Anthony Coltrale was murdered in Watts by a Los Angeles officer.

Mindful of FBI repression, the Panthers pressed on. Eldridge Cleaver led the way by establishing a coalition with the Peace and Freedom Party (PFP), a young white political party. Earl Anthony attended one meeting with Eldridge to map out the coalition agenda. Cleaver said that each group should have different roles, since they each had different problems. Only black people would speak on behalf of black folks and the same for whites. Finally, the coalition would help both groups achieve their goals.

Seale was adamant that the PFP had to support the "Free Huey" campaign, and they agreed. Cleaver wrote a statement "Revolution in the White Mother County and National Liberation in the Black Colony" for the March 16, 1968 Peace and Freedom Party's founding convention. The PFP donated three thousand dollars to the Huey Newton defense fund. While Panther footsoldiers sold *The Black Panther*, they also generated interest in the PFP.

Previous page: **P**lastic pig with knife in its side found in the New Bedford, Massachusetts, Black Panther headquarters after it was raided by the police.

Above: **J. Edgar Hoover**

Right: **Kathleen Cleaver**

Because the PFP was a new political party, it needed candidates to run for office. It reluctantly invited three Party members to fill their slates for the November election. Huey was selected to run for Congress in the 7th Congressional District of Alameda County, Bobby Seale for the 17th Assembly District, and Kathleen Cleaver for the 18th Assembly seat in San Francisco. On August 18, 1968, Eldridge was nominated as the presidential candidate on the Peace and Freedom Party ticket. Cleaver won more votes than his competitors: Dr. Benjamin Spock, Senator Eugene McCarthy, and Dick Gregory. However, the Constitution requires a U.S. president to be at least thirty-five years. So Cleaver was ineligible. At election time the PFP had no chance of shifting the Republican tide. Richard Nixon and his scandalous entourage swept the election. Even in jail, however, Huey Newton managed to chalk up 25,000 votes.

Some black folks were not jubilant about the Party's coalition with the PFP, fearing that white liberals would dilute the essence of the Party by alienating the black community. Cleaver described a visit to Los Angeles with Seale and other Panthers: "We were really put through a lot of changes by black cats who didn't relate to the Peace and Freedom Party. They told us rather frankly that we had become tools of the white racists." Law enforcement agencies also were not thrilled by the Party's coalition with PFP. Oakland police harassed, without probable cause, Panther women and men putting up posters for Panther candidates on the PFP ticket. Oakland residents reported seeing officers tearing down campaign posters.

To Hoover's FBI, the combined efforts of the PFP and the Panthers reeked of a communist connection. The Party membership had long been accused of being the arm of Fidel Castro and the Communist Party U.S.A. Racist America didn't believe black men and women, on their own, could effectively organize against police harassment and political oppression. Hoover was determined to neutralize any threat by the "Reds" to take control of the United States. With the assassination of Dr. Martin Luther King Jr. on April 4, 1968, his task became easier.

Dr. King's murder at the Lorraine Motel in Memphis, Tennessee ignited riots in major cities across the country, yet Oakland remained calm because of the efforts of the Black Panther Party. Members equipped with megaphones strapped to the top of cars drove through black neighborhoods urging residents to be cool and attend their rally on April 7 at Defermery Park. Local radio stations broadcast news about the rally/picnic, and the police were aware of the Oakland Panthers' agenda to organize mournful black people into a crescendo of Panthers.

The day before the rally, over fifty Oakland and Emeryville police officers ambushed Bobby Hutton (17), Eldridge Cleaver (33), David Hilliard (25), Donnell Lankford (18), Wendell Wade (23), Terry Cotton (21), John L. Scott (17) and Warren Wells (21) at 1218 28th Street in Oakland. The ninety-minute gun battle unleashed an estimated one thousand rounds of ammunition into the basement where Cleaver and Hutton hid for cover. When the officers ordered them to "Throw out your weapons!" several guns came flying out of windows. Cleaver and Hutton emerged from a basement flooded with tear gas

1968: BALLOT OR THE BULLET

and set on fire. Both Wells and Cleaver were wounded, and Hutton was killed "by a volley of pigs' bullets as he surrendered with his arms above his head." At least six policemen shot Hutton in the back at point-blank range. Cleaver survived the attack because he had removed all his clothes and walked out of the house with his hands above his head. The police could not say he was carrying a weapon. Hutton, however, only removed his shirt and was not spared. Cleaver credits the many "beautiful black people crowded around demanding that the cops not shoot" him with saving his life. The police arrested the seven surviving Panthers and set bail for Cleaver at sixty-three thousand dollars. But his parole was immediately revoked and he was incarcerated. All other Panthers were held on $40,000 bail. One black police officer present resigned from the force in disgust.

The rally went on as scheduled, the largest turnout ever, in tribute to Lil' Bobby Hutton. At the rally black citizens learned that, initially, the officers shot at the home of three sisters—Victoria Battiste (75), Melvina Jones (77), and Ophelia Jones (82) located at 1206 28th street. After Mrs. Battiste got up to put on her robe, a bullet hit over her bed. The cops entered and left their home without an apology. Police Chief Charles Gains delivered a forty-five minute message on television against the Panthers:

The Black Panther party poses a real threat to the peace and tranquillity of the city of Oakland. Calling the police murderers, calling them Fascist pigs, and claiming the police do not protect and police the minority community is ridiculous on its face. It is both ridiculous and irrational. The Black Panther party has no

Below: **Eldridge Cleaver being guarded in an ambulance by Officer Rick Reid while waiting for transfer from hospital to prison. Cleaver had been wounded in the leg by the Oakland police in April 1968.**

Opposite: **The house, gas-filled and set afire by police, where Hutton was murdered and Cleaver wounded in police attack.**

practical, implementable programs to my knowledge and it's about time that all reasonable persons in the city of Oakland, both black and white, recognize the Black Panther party for what it is and let them know that the people in this city are not going to tolerate their unlawful activities and their irrationality. This must be done if we are going to have peace in this city.

Chief Gains was followed by his colleague Oakland mayor John Readings, who said that he had once tried to help Negroes, but he was reconsidering that position.

*A noisy and illogical demand is made for the release of Huey
Newton, who was apprehended and indicted by the Grand Jury
on the charge of killing an Oakland police officer. Let me
assure you that this city government will insist that this charge
be pressed with vigor and determination by the District
Attorney's office....There is also a maudlin hue and cry about
the recent death of Bobby Hutton, but we have heard little of the
four police officers who were shot.*

Gains and Readings dismissed the fact that their remarks were
prejudicial to the jury. In the end, the Oakland grand jury, all white,
middle-class citizens, defended the police conduct and found Hutton's killing "justified." The Panthers made efforts to get the FBI and
other agencies of the Justice Department to investigate the murder,
but nothing was done.

Ironically, many officers believed that they were performing their
job well and within the law. One Oakland officer stated, "I don't
think I'm prejudiced—not the way some guys are here. Sure I call
them 'niggers' around the department—everyone does it, so I do it,
too. But I don't let my kids say nigger at home." Another Oakland
policeman confessed, "It's harder to work in these [black] neighborhoods now than it used to be because we send the kids to school
and teach them about rights and then put them back in the neigh-

borhood. I think we ought to either get rid of these neighborhoods or stop teaching these kids about their rights."

On April 11, the black community came out in full force in support of the Panthers and declined to give credence to Oakland Chief Gains' version of the April 6 ambush. A group called Blacks Strike for Justice was organized under the leadership of Paul Cobb, a member of the West Oakland Planning Committee. Since the political/legal apparatus refused to reprimand the police, the groups planned to strike back at the Oakland establishment through the pocketbook. They began a boycott against businesses that had racist policies and hired no black people. Protest signs read "Don't Shop Here, Walk On By." Fifty percent of their business was lost overnight. Conservative black people who had shunned the Panthers now closed ranks. White Oakland's response to the boycott was predictable and immediate. The *Oakland Tribune,* owned by William Knowland, branded the boycott an exercise in extortion.

Black moderates who had previously shunned the party were also appalled by the actions of local police agencies. Dr. Carlton Goodlett, editor and publisher of the *Oakland Sun-Reporter,* argued in "Protect the Panthers," that "We vigorously condemn the violation of the constitutional rights of the Black Panther Party, and of all other black citizens, by the organized police forces of Berkeley, Oakland, and San Francisco." Goodlett was also critical that

> *The failure of black professionals and bourgeoisie to speak out in protest against their police establishment's systematic and apparently purposeful drive to cut down the black militant groups implies a conspiracy of silence....How long must the voice of a united black community remain muted or silent on this dangerous threat to the personal freedom and liberties of us all?*

The support from Black moderates was a welcome change from their previous silence.

On April 13, more than twenty-five hundred people mourned at Hutton's funeral at the Ephesian Church of God in Christ. Bobby Seale spoke and also read a tribute to Lil' Bobby written by Huey Newton, who was still in jail after the Officer Frey incident. Five ministers, including George Murray, minister of education for the Party and Rev. Earl Neil, eulogized Hutton. Rev. E. E. Cleveland gave a moving and militant address, speaking at length of the hog in the stream, saying, "the water had been pure and clean, but had become tainted and muddy." He asserted that the "stream needed to be cleaned of the pigs so that everyone could get a fresh drink of water."

Following the funeral, more than two thousand people attended a tribute to Hutton at Lakeside Park in Oakland. Marlon Brando, who had attended the funeral, stated over the loudspeaker: "That could have been my son lying there. It's up to each individual to do something. I've got a lot to learn. I haven't suffered the way you have suffered." A memorial rally was also held in front of the bullet-ridden scene of the crime. The house looked like it had been sent to Vietnam and back, a scene of overkill. The air smelled of the stench of tear-gas fumes and fire smoke, while the concrete was stained with the blood of Hutton. Four Panthers were sprayed with Mace and arrested after leaving the Hutton procession, on suspicion of robbery. The struggle continued.

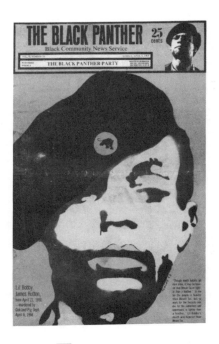

Above: The front page of *The Black Panther* after Bobby Hutton's murder.

Opposite top: Actor Marlon Brando with Black Panthers at the funeral for Lil' Bobby Hutton, April 15, 1968.

Opposite bottom: Members of the Brown Berets, a Chicano group, who supported the Panthers and the "Free Huey" campaign.

On May 2, 1968, the Panthers filed a federal civil suit in San Francisco against the city of Oakland (Mayor John Reading, Police Chief Charles Gains, Officer Herbert Heanes, and District Attorney J. Frank Coakley) to stop systematic attempts to harass, intimidate, and demolish the Black Panther Party. The suit reported the use of "alley court" terrorist tactics and placing guns to the heads of Panthers to extract phony confessions. The suit also detailed how it was impossible for Huey to receive a fair trial because of the methods used to select grand juries in California. Justice Spurgeon Avakian acknowledged that black people in California were disqualified for grand jury duty at the rate of over 80 percent because of the screening test. Black people with complaints were forced to appeal to a hostile district attorney and a racist police department. In May 1968, out of 647 Oakland police officers, 22 were black, and only 2 black men were in command positions, of captain and sergeant. The lawsuit attacked institutional racism within the legal and political systems.

By May 20, 1968, Cleaver applied in the Superior Court for a writ of habeas corpus. He stated that from the time he joined the Nation of Islam in 1960 while incarcerated at San Quentin Prison, he was "consistently persecuted, hounded, and harassed by the Department of Correction and the Adult Authority of California because he is black, and an active, vocal, and militant defender of the oppressed black people of the nation." As Cleaver appealed for release, other Panthers, rotating periods of incarceration, worked against the organization's morale and treasury. By June 1968 Panther Charles Bursey

Below: **T**he Philadelphia Police raided a house they said was a Panther Headquarters on March 11, 1970.

Opposite: **Members of the Black Panthers at the United Nations in New York.**

had lived as a political prisoner in the "hole" (naked, no running water, no toilet, no lights, no mattress, green mush for meals). He suffered seizures and was given no medical attention. Bursey died years later from a head tumor. On June 11, 1968, Judge Raymond Sherwin surprisingly granted Cleaver's writ of habeas corpus. Sherwin ruled in an extraordinary opinion:

> *The uncontradicted evidence presented to the court indicated that the petitioner had been a model parolee.*
> *The peril to his parole status stemmed from no failure of personal rehabilitation but from his undue eloquence in pursing political goals, goals which were offensive to many of his contemporaries. Not only was there absence of cause for the cancellation of parole, it was the product of a type of pressure unbecoming to say the least, to the law enforcement paraphernalia of this state.*

Eldridge Cleaver was released on a twenty-five-dollar bond the following day, but not without a fifty-thousand-dollar bail. The bail bond company took five thousand dollars in cash and Paul Jacobs, Dr. Jane Aguilar, Godfrey Cambridge, Dr. Phillip Shapiro, and Ed Keaton provided the collateral for the remainder of the money. Keating drove Eldridge from the jail and remembered suddenly hearing Eldridge roar, "Goddamn! I can't believe it! I'm free."

Once "free," Cleaver immediately continued his attack against the injustices that plagued the United States. He led an entourage of Panthers to the United Nations on June 25, 1968. They protested Newton's incarceration as a political prisoner and the genocidal

Opposite above: **H**uey Newton manacled at his trial in the Alameda County Court House.

Above: Spectators in Los Angeles watch police drive 11 Panthers from their barracaded building on December 8, 1969.

Opposite below: Newton's supporters demonstrate outside the Alameda County Court House.

actions of the U.S. government against African Americans. The power of African liberation from colonial rule facilitated African American liberation in a number of ways. Most importantly, for the first time black people had a voice in the United Nations.

Panthers were not the only activists in the Bay Area protesting against the "system." On June 30, 1968, Berkeley mayor Wallace J. S. Johnson enacted a citywide curfew after a third night of rioting by antidraft protesters. Six persons were arrested on charges ranging from firebombing to curfew violation and looting; more than 40 were injured. More than seven hundred police officers and sheriffs' deputies from Oakland and surrounding cities were called in to "keep the peace."

In the midst of this melee Panthers managed another victory. They opened an additional Party office in West Oakland, led by Tommy Jones and Glen Stafford. Panthers not only remodeled and painted the interior and exterior of the dilapidated building but also cleaned the apartments above the storefront office where senior citizens lived, and daily provided them with meals.

On July 15, 1968, Huey P. Newton's trial began. The Alameda County Courthouse was tightly secured. More than 5,000 protesters and about 450 Panthers came out in support of Newton on the steps of the courthouse. A mixed crowd of black, Chicano, white, young, and old thundered "Free Huey now!" The newly formed Brown

Berets, Chicano activists, also made their appearance on the court-house steps; the Chicanos were clad in khaki shirts, brown pants, and brown berets. Gene McKinney was astonished by the turnout. After the Officer Frey shootout he left his IBM job and went back to Philadelphia. Gene remarked: "When I left it wasn't too many people who was for the Party. But after I came back, maybe because of the incident down on Seventh Street, everybody you see has a black leather jacket and a tam cap, old ladies and little kids. It was for real. It was alive. I said, Damn! Everybody's found it now. Right on!"

Charles Garry's strategy was to explain to jurors the philosophy of the Black Panthers and how the organization had become a symbol, in the eyes of the police department, as public enemy No. 1. Garry discussed evidence of continual harassment of Newton and "the cry in the police department: Get Huey Newton! Get rid of him! Off!" Garry never elaborated on the details of the shooting. Instead, he talked about Newton's wounds and the brutality of the police. The establishment hated Huey because of his uncompromising stand against the abuse of power by officers throughout black urban communities. Garry discussed Newton as the victim of a frame-up. The Oakland police department, assisted by the media, painted a picture of Newton as a violent demon who required containment. In a prison interview Huey said that he was "absolutely against violence. Violence indicates aggression. I am for self-defense. Self-defense is a declaration against violence."

Numerous Panthers and community members testified. Luther Smith spoke about Officer Frey's conduct, saying he was verbally abusive, used racial slurs, threats, constant harassments, insults, and physical abuse. Gene McKinney pled the Fifth Amendment in response to questions about the shooting. He was given six months for refusing to testify. Garry's strategy was to cast a reasonable doubt in the jurors' minds that Gene, not Huey, shot Frey.

As the Newton trial continued throughout the month of August, Panthers and Party offices were venomously attacked. At the West Oakland office, Matilaba had painted a mural on the back wall of a Panther holding a gun. The police busted down the door, overturned desks, emptied drawers, destroyed papers, and shot at the mural. They claimed they mistook the mural for someone standing in the rear of the office with a gun. No arrests were made. The Newark Panther office was firebombed; the Detroit Panthers exchanged a head-up shoot-out with police, but there were no injuries. Seattle Panthers were harassed and arrested for concealed weapons. Los Angeles was the hardest hit: Three Panthers—Robert Lawrence, Steve Bartholomew, and Tommy Lewis—were murdered by policemen. More than fifty bullets and shotgun blasts hit their car as they stopped at a gas station.

The FBI also obstructed the mobility of Panthers, who could barely walk the streets. Officers collected names, and license plate numbers, took photos, and wrote descriptions. Oakland Panthers David Hilliard, George Murray, and Landon Williams were prevented from traveling to Cuba from Mexico. The *San Francisco Chronicle* carried an article exposing Panther George Murray as a teacher at San Francisco State. The chancellor ordered Murray's termination. Outraged, the campus Black Student Union went on strike. Kathleen Cleaver,

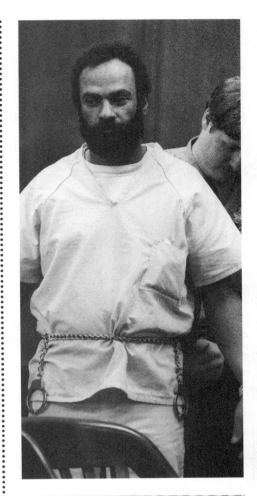

ALAMEDA COUNTY

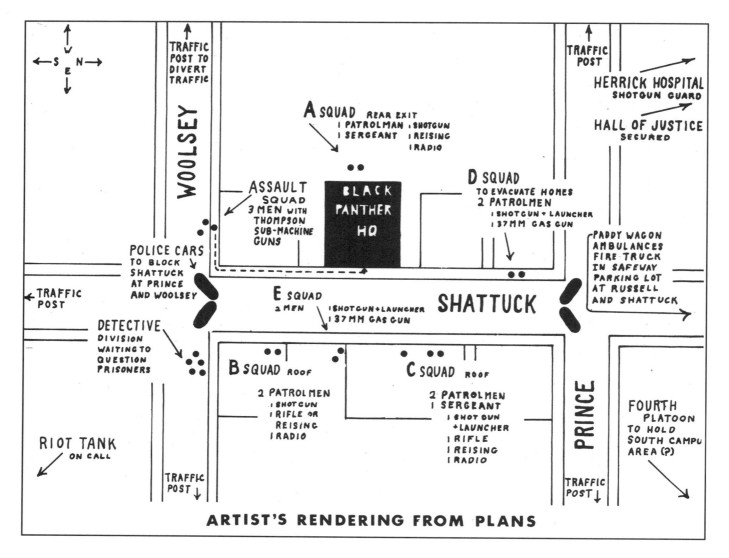

Above: **M**ap prepared by Berkeley police as a contingency plan to raid Black Panther headquarters, August 30, 1969.

Right: A police swat team launches an attack on the Los Angeles Panther headquarters in December 1969.

serving as the Party's communication secretary, and Earl Anthony were refused entry into Japan from Hawaii. Kathleen had attended the founding convention of the Peace and Freedom Party in Hawaii and had been invited to a speaking tour in Japan. Somehow, some way, the Panthers gathered strength from their ancestors and pressed onward. Hilliard and Seale attended the 1968 National Democratic Convention in Chicago, speaking to crowds of nearly five thousand across the street from the convention. This convention was marked by a four-day riot.

On September 8, after four days of deliberation, the Newton jury came up with a "compromise" verdict. Huey was convicted of voluntary manslaughter and acquitted of the assault and kidnap charges. Four hours after the Newton decision, two on-duty, admittedly drunk Oakland officers drove by the Panther office on Grove Street and fired shots at the posters of Newton and Cleaver taped on the windows. They also shot five bullets into the apartments above the office where citizens slept. Police Chief Gains only verbally reprimanded the officers and said that "…they were only blowing off a little steam…." J. Edgar Hoover declared on September 11, 1968, that the Black Panther Party was "the greatest threat to the internal security of the country."

On September 27, 1968, Huey Newton was sentenced by a jury composed of "seven women and five men, one Negro, one Japanese-American and one Spanish-American," to 2 to 15 years for manslaughter. On this same day the Court of Appeals ordered Cleaver to return to jail. He was granted a sixty-day stay until November 26, 1968. Cleaver vowed not to return to jail, and continued to lecture across the country. The University of California at Berkeley hosted a series of his lectures. On October 1, 1968, Governor Ronald Reagan stated that Cleaver should not be allowed to give lectures on the campus. Superintendent of Education Max Rafferty refused to pay Eldridge's salary. State Senator John Schmitz sponsored a bill to withhold the university's budget if Cleaver was not fired at once. Cleaver reacted by presenting a lecture on October 9. On the steps of Sproul Hall, near the Sather Gate where Panthers sold Chairman Mao's *Quotations,* he led over five thousand students in a chorus of "Fuck Ronald Reagan!" On October 15, a warrant was issued for Eldridge's arrest.

UC Berkeley students demonstrated against the university's reluctance to give them credit for Cleaver's special lecture course—Social Analysis 139X. When the students refused to leave, they were arrest-

ed by forty Alameda County "pigs." After Cleaver did not appear for his November 27, 1968 hearing, Judge Folger Emerson ordered his fifty thousand dollar bail forfeited and due to the court by June 20. The six-person committee who guaranteed Eldridge's bail stated, "The committee has no regrets about Cleaver's action and we accept our responsibility for the ransom payment and we hope the community at large will help share our financial burden." Cleaver left the United States on November 26 for Cuba via Montreal, Canada. He arrived in Havana on December 25, 1968. He lived in Havana under guard for seven months and then settled in Algeria, where he and Kathleen established an international section of the Black Panther Party. Prior to joining Eldridge, Kathleen gave a New York radio address that was reprinted in the *Black Panther Party*. She stated, "The most outstanding problem that the black community and in particular the Black Panther Party as a vanguard of the Liberation Struggle will have to deal with in the coming months of 1969 will be the black bootlicker, the puppet placed on black people by the white pig power structure to suppress us."

Hoover and local officers anticipated the direction of the Party and set up barriers to its success by the use of agents provocateurs. Hoover kept track of state and city police activity by crime statistics compiled and submitted to his office yearly. He watched the rise and fall of reported crime and arrests and located his agents accordingly. As the Party's membership expanded, it was easier for FBI agents to infiltrate chapters. In November 1968 Hoover sent a message to all his field agents "to exploit all avenues of creating…dissension within the ranks of the BPP…recipient offices are instructed to submit imaginative and hard-hitting counterintelligence measures aimed at crippling the BPP." Between 1967 and 1971 Hoover's domestic counterintelligence Program (COINTELPRO) aggressively sought to stifle the growth of the Party. In 1971 COINTELPRO was "suspended" because the FBI feared "embarrassment to the bureau" in light of media exposure of its clandestine activities. In reality, it was folded into other FBI departments.

COINTELPRO employed secret, often illegal campaigns to repress "undesirable" individuals or organizations, particularly in the 1960s. Its surveillance included mail tampering and creation of documents — fabricated letters and bogus propaganda (cartoons, rumors) — between groups and individuals to instigate internal dissension, splits, and violent reprisal. Dummy letters detailing extra-marital affairs were even sent to spouses to break up Panther marriages. Wiretaps, burglaries, and tails were also used for surveillance—not to accumulate evidence but to instill paranoia. The FBI successfully replaced loyalty with suspicion and turned former comrades into enemies.

Most FBI informers and agents provocateurs were ex-convicts with long criminal records of arrests and convictions but with little time served. They exchanged long prison time for probation and undercover work. The agents were assigned various duties, including initiating illegal activities that could be blamed on legitimate members of the Party. They generated suspicion around a particular member to isolate and perhaps eliminate him or her. Informer William O'Neal became the chief of security for the Chicago chapter and bodyguard to Chairman Fred Hampton. Between 1969 and 1972 O'Neal was paid over thirty thousand dollars and provided a car allowance. Hoover had more than seven thousand "racial informants," sixty-seven in the Black Panther Party.

On May 20, 1968 the *San Francisco Chronicle* featured an article by Charles Howe, "Secret Agent's Analysis of the Panthers," based on a two-week investigation. The agent, called Marsh, stated that it was easy to penetrate the Party; their ability to screen out potential spies was "not the best." He reported the Panthers' level of paramilitary training as low, the quality of weapons as "inadequate." Marsh confirmed that "the arms are lawfully purchased on a retail basis, we believe the Panthers are not yet sophisticated to understand volume purchasing, which can be done wholesale from a federal firearms dealer's stamp. Such a stamp may be obtained from anyone not convicted of a felony." Marsh continued, "If conditions get rougher in the ghetto—any ghetto—they're going to get more recruits. Then a hard-core element may escalate the gun business again. If the federal government, on the other hand, makes a serious effort to pump lots of money into the ghetto, you can likely kiss the Panthers goodbye. You simply can't agitate happy people."

It was never clear if a "Panther" was actually an agent, but when behavior was suspicious it could not be ruled out. The Bay Area had

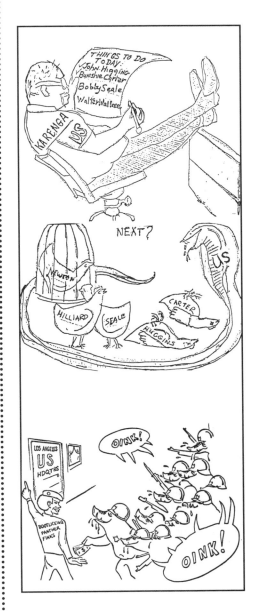

Opposite above: **E**ldridge **Cleaver, in center, on the Berkeley University of California campus.**

Opposite below and above: **Cartoons produced and sent out by the Los Angeles FBI office as part of the COINTELPRO campaign to provoke tension between the Black Panthers and Ron Karenga's US.**

its first major setup from an agent on November 19, 1968. Eight Panthers were arrested in San Francisco after a service station holdup in which gunfire was exchanged with police. A white van with a sign, "The Black Panther Black Community News Service," pulled into Gene Goodwin's gas station. Goodwin saw two men in the van. One passenger followed his attendant to receive change for the gas purchase. At the cash box, the passenger pulled a gun on the attendant and robbed him of eighty dollars. The attendant was surprised to see another van passenger casually walk to the rest room and return as if he had no clue about what was going on. The robber walked back to the van, and the driver slowly left the station. Goodwin recalled that he had more than enough time to write down the license plate numbers. That afternoon the same van passed police headquarters in San Francisco. As the driver was being checked out, gunfire erupted from inside the van. An officer and a Panther were seriously wounded. All Panthers were arrested but charges were dismissed against all but one of the Panthers, whom the Party accused of being an agent provocateur and later expelled.

The experience of Agent Earl Anthony reveals much about the FBI and the Black Panther Party. Anthony graduated from the University of Southern California as a member of the Young Republicans. He moved to San Francisco to attend law school. He dabbled in progressive activism at Hunter's Point. Anthony's initial visits from FBI agents Robert O' Connor and Ron Kizenski were quite friendly and harmless. The agents were his former college football teammates. Anthony had become attracted to the Party because they were "bold" and a "step ahead" of other black liberation organizations. He approached Eldridge Cleaver, who was impressed that Anthony was in his last year of law school. Cleaver took him to meet Bobby Seale, who had to approve his membership. Earl Anthony was accepted into the Party in April 1967. He traveled with the Panthers to Richmond to protest the murder of Denzil Dowell. He had never seen black men "command the respect of the people" the way Seale and Newton had. Anthony was as surprised as everyone else when the Panthers "invaded" Sacramento. He had not been invited to attend. However, soon Anthony was named captain of the San Francisco area.

The FBI came to Anthony's apartment on July 7, 1967, on the pretext of questioning him on his whereabouts at the time the selective service draft board was bombed in Van Nuys, California. Anthony had dropped out of law school, and the draft board tried to reclassify his status. At his draft board hearing he wore Panther attire. At the end of August 1967, he was paid another visit by Robert O'Connor and Ron Kizenski, who no longer played their college buddy role. The agents told Earl they believed he had something to do with the bombing, but they were willing to cut him a deal. "They would not charge me if I were to become an informant for the FBI inside the Black Panther Party." Earl laughed; they beat him until he was unconscious. When Earl woke he agreed to become an informer. He was to meet with the agents every Tuesday at the beach, or they would contact him. Soon the agents brought up his past political activity at Hunter's Point. Apparently there had been a shoot-out and murder of two housing authority police at Hunter's Point. The agents

Above and opposite: **B**lack Panther truck said to be involved in a gas station holdup and exchange of gunfire with police in San Francisco, November 19, 1968.

threatened to implicate him in that killing. "I knew the FBI had me hooked." Initially, the FBI's plan of action was to get Earl to convince Cleaver to start warfare with cultural nationalists. However, this campaign failed in the Bay Area. Panthers had disagreements with cultural nationalists, but they understood the importance of African American history and culture and respected these brothers and sisters. The agents then told Earl to ask Cleaver to transfer him to the new chapter in Los Angeles. In January 1968, Anthony was sent to Los Angeles to assist Bunchy Carter. Anthony was once again instructed to start ideological warfare but this time with Ron Karenga's group, United Slaves (US).

Charismatic and articulate, Karenga attracted brothers and sisters from the community who supported his cultural nationalist agenda. His signature shaven head and dashiki attire were replicated by his male members. Tensions between the Panthers and US stemmed back to the "Free Huey" rally in February 1968. US had accused the Party of making slanderous comments about Karenga, and they wanted an apology. Bunchy and Earl clarified that the Party had not disrespected Karenga, and the meeting ended on an upbeat note. However, as the Panthers became US's rival for membership, tensions again became evident. Bunchy recruited from the Teen Post where he worked as a counselor. The numbers of Los Angeles Panthers reached more than two hundred. The FBI began to send dummy letters to Karenga, stating that the Panthers were going to kill him, and to circulate unflattering cartoons.

By December 1968, US and the Panthers disagreed over the appointment of the director of black studies at the University of California at Los Angeles (UCLA). Karenga sought the appointment. The Panthers and the BSU thought the new director should have many attributes including a Ph.D. Karenga had only an M.A., and the chancellor yielded to the Panther-BSU point of view. Informers Earl Anthony and Louis Tackwood stated the agents "worked out a deal with Karenga where they would supply US with weapons and a master plan to destroy the L.A. Black Panthers."

A meeting was scheduled for February 17, 1969, to resolve issues between US and the Panthers. Both groups agreed to come unarmed and peaceful, but when they arrived, John Huggins and Bunchy Carter, both students at UCLA, were murdered in the Campbell Hall lunchroom. Former FBI agent Darthard Perry said in a sworn affidavit that he saw US members Larry (Ali) Steiner and George Steiner "execute" Bunchy in the chest and John in the back with .357 Magnums. After the murder the police invaded the home of John Huggins and arrested seventeen Panthers, including John's wife, Erica, with their ten-day-old baby. These Panthers were charged with conspiracy to commit murder. Three days later, FBI agents called for another round of cartoons to "indicate to the BPP that the US organization feels they are ineffectual, inadequate, and riddled with graft and corruption." The FBI was successful in duping US members into ambushing Carter and Huggins. At the trial Agent Louis Tackwood testified that Karenga received police subsidies in the form of money, drugs, and weapons to attack Party members. Four US followers along with the Steiner brothers were

Opposite: **M**ass demonstration on steps of Los Angeles City Hall by Black Panthers protesting the national pattern of police raids on Panther headquarters. Leaders of African American organizations had called for a strike by black residents to protest the December 8, 1969 four-hour police siege of the LA Panther headquarters.

convicted of the murders and imprisoned in San Quentin.

The FBI believed that with Eldridge and Huey gone and Bunchy murdered, they could crush the Panthers. Anthony had kept a journal on his experiences as a Panther, which the FBI told him to publish. They believed that a book would be Anthony's vehicle to party leadership. Cleaver was totally against his writing a book, and placed Anthony under house arrest at David Hilliard's for being an opportunist. However, Earl was "more afraid of his 'friends' in the FBI than I was of any Panther threat." In March Anthony went to Paris. The March 29, 1969, edition of *The Black Panther* viciously attacked Anthony and officially purged him from the Party. When Earl came back to the United States in December 1969, the FBI

> *suggested that I move back to San Francisco and become a drug dealer; I moved back to San Francisco and became a drug dealer. They yelled "jump" and I asked them "how high." I grew tired and wanted out, demanded out. And that was when the real nightmare started…. to fight the social revolution in this country is like "spitting in the wind; it will fly back into your face."*

No state where Panthers organized was exempt from the FBI assault. In Des Moines, Iowa, more than a hundred police stormed the Party office in a home and harassed members on January 30, 1969. But the members went on working for the movement. So on March 26, 1969, the office was demolished by explosives. Fortunately, all six occupants survived, but two were severely injured. Forty-eight other homes in a three-block radius suffered damage. The speedy arrival of police at the scene created suspicion among the witnesses.

Officers arrested Panthers for allegedly bombing their own headquarters. Two days later, in San Francisco, the police raided the Panther office with M-16 Thompson submachine guns and .30-caliber carbines. All sixteen Panthers in the office were tear-gassed, fired upon, and arrested. In thirty minutes they were released without charges. On April 1, 1969, twenty-one New York Panthers were arrested on a wide variety of conspiracy charges, including bomb threats to department stores, police stations, the Bronx Botanical Garden, and a section of railroad tracks. They became known as the New York 21. In Chicago, on April 13, 1969, the FBI set up an elaborate scheme to arrest four Panthers—Nathaniel Junior, William McClinton, Jr., Merril Harvey, and Michael White. An agent posed as an illicit gun dealer and faked the sale to the Panthers while officers perched on surrounding rooftops; others watched from trailer trucks equipped with high-powered weapons and floodlights.

On April 17, 1969, Hoover testified before the House Subcommittee on Appropriations that certain groups were not civil rights organizations but "preach hatred for the white race, demand immunity from laws, and advocate violence, constitute a serious threat to our country's internal security….Government has made it necessary for the FBI to intensify its intelligence operations in this field." The Justice Department implemented a special Panther Task Force "to develop a prosecutive theory against the BPP." The unit specifically examined Panthers' financial affairs, including the personal income of individuals. It even conducted "a survey to determine how many members are on welfare."

Opposite: **D**emonstrators jam the Los Angeles Hall of Justice lobby to protest police harassment of Black Panthers.

Below: Demonstrators outside the Alameda County Courthouse at the time of Huey Newton's trial.

Black Panthers in New York City were infiltrated by an FBI agent provocateur in August 1969. Three Panthers were arrested and charged with conspiracy to rob a hotel, conspiracy to murder, attempted robbery, attempted murder of an officer at the scene of the arrest, and possession of weapons. The agent drew a map of the hotel and then suggested that the Panthers rob it. He also offered to obtain guns for the Panthers. After a lengthy trial the jury found that the three Panthers had been entrapped and acquitted them of all charges except possession of a sawed-off shotgun.

On August 14, 1969, US members wounded two Panthers and killed Panther Sylvester Bell in San Diego, California. The following day the FBI affirmed its "success" and stated: "In view of the recent killing of BPP member Sylvester Bell, a new cartoon is being considered in hopes that it will assist in the continuance of the rift between the BPP and US." The Panthers retaliated by bombing US offices. Karenga admitted that the FBI "interjected the violence into it…the normal rivalries of two groups struggling for leadership of the black movement."

William O'Neal in Chicago had a long list of arrests, including car theft and impersonating a federal officer. Agent Roy Martin Mitchell got O'Neal to agree to a monthly stipend to penetrate the Chicago chapter in late 1968 if the charges were dropped. Fred Hampton, leader of the Chicago chapter was an effective organizer who inspired confidence in the people. On January 24, 1969, the Chicago police and the FBI conspired to prevent him from appearing on a TV talk show. The FBI feared that he would rise up in the national leadership ranks and thought he had to be eliminated. O'Neal gave agents daily reports on the activities of the chapter and Party leadership. By February he became Hampton's personal bodyguard and received a pay raise from three hundred dollars to six hundred dollars per month from the FBI.

At this point O'Neal aggressively initiated a flood of arrests of Chicago Panthers. On March 3, 1969, O'Neal was arrested along with Bobby Rush, Nathaniel Junior, and Saundra Rich for possession of narcotics. Their bail was set at $1,000 each. On April 26, 1969, Fred Hampton and fifteen other Party members were indicted by the grand jury on such charges as stealing ice cream and distributing it to neighborhood children, kidnapping, and unlawful use of weapons. On June 10, 1969, O'Neal and sixteen other Panthers were arrested for conspiracy, kidnapping, and aggravated battery. Bail was set at $100,000 each. On June 17, 1969, O'Neal was arrested with Robert Bruce for possession of narcotics. William O'Neal was an excellent informer because he satisfied the FBI's goal to deplete the Party's treasury and keep the Panthers off the streets.

O'Neal provided the FBI with a floor-plan of Hampton's apartment, which included details on where weapons were in the house. On December 4, 1969, he drugged Hampton, and that night the police assassinated Hampton and Panther Mark Clark (17). Ninety bullets were shot into the apartment within a ten-minute period. The Chicago police smiled as they carried Hampton's body out on a stretcher. Prior to the funerals, O'Neal went to Hampton's parents' home and began the rumor that an FBI agent was in the apartment on the morning of the massacre. O'Neal was given a three-hundred-dollar bonus for a job well done.

Despite the deadly police attacks on Panthers in August 1970, the U.S. Senate Un-American Activities Subcommittee claimed the Black Panthers were "controlled" by the Communist Party for use as revolutionary "shock troops." The report contended that the U.S. Communist Party had provided the guidance and inspiration for the Oakland-based Party. The report estimated Panther strength at 25,000 and claimed members had become "more boldly militant and violated the law with growing contempt." According to the report, Panthers were "stockpiling supplies of weapons and ammunition, patrolling streets, and acting as an armed guerrilla force....It would be useless for us to attempt any description of the psychotic hatred for all law enforcement officers that exists in the Panther organization." In reality, the Panthers were not against "policing" but they wanted the black community to be controlled by officers who lived among them. They believed that if a man lived in the community, he would know the people and not unjustly brutalize residents.

In New Orleans, police raided the Panthers' headquarters on September 15, 1970. After a gunfire exchange, one Panther was killed and three others were wounded. Fourteen Panthers were arrested and charged with attempted murder. Prior to the raid, the New Orleans Panthers had filed suit against the police department in Federal District Court to stop their harassment of members who sold *The Black Panther*. They had been charged with peddling without a license, despite a law that unlicensed vendors could not be arrested.

The Panthers' few victories kept them going. The federal district court in Oregon found that the Portland police violated the civil rights of Captain Kent Ford of the Party by beating him while he was in custody. Two witnesses also in custody saw the beating and testified. Ford was beaten while handcuffed. The court awarded him $1,000 in compensatory damages and $5,000 in punitive damages. The court stated, "The people of the community cannot be expected to have confidence in the government until the government's officers act fairly and according to law toward all members of the community."

The FBI tried hard to turn Panthers into criminals, although the ferocity of Hoover's attack varied from case to case. By 1969 the Panthers had more than 5,000 members. More than 3,000 of them were arrested at some point because of FBI and police efforts to neutralize the Party.

This activity had a profound impact on Party morale and unity. Too many members became reckless and undisciplined. Abuse of power translated into terrorist behavior—Panthers killing Panthers. The Party argued that African Americans had no channel to seek redress against police invasion and harassment. Unfortunately, they failed to implement channels in their own organization. If a Panther was accused or suspected of being an informer or exhibiting "counterrevolutionary, opportunist behavior," he or she was expelled. If a Panther spoke out against the leadership or complained about abuse, the member was purged. How could the Party survive and thrive under this weight?

Opposite: **B**ullet holes fired by police through Panther headquarters window into images of Newton and Cleaver.

Above: **Fred Hampton, leader of the Chicago Panther chapter.**

GROWING PAINS

Despite the dangers associated with the Black Panther Party, African Americans continued to join its ranks. By late 1968, the Party was armed with workers willing to implement various points of the organization's ten-point program. The Party's Central Committee, the decision-making body of the organization, under the leadership of Chairman Seale, elected to create community- based programs. Huey explained in his book *To Die for the People,* "We recognize that in order to bring the people to the level of consciousness where they would seize the time, it would be necessary to serve their interests in survival by developing programs which would help them to meet their daily needs."

The Party aimed to gain complete control of the institutions in the community. They hoped their programs would have a threefold effect: meet the immediate needs of the citizens they pledged to serve; inspire the African American community to take up guns to defend the programs; and demonstrate that the Party did so much with so little while the government did so little with so much. This would help community members demand from the government what they needed for a decent livelihood. These programs also freed the Party from criticism that they had no legitimate activities. Aligning themselves with local churches, the Party introduced its Free Breakfast for Children Program (FBCP) in January 1969.

The Party's FBCP began at St. Augustine Church under the guidance of Huey's spiritual adviser and the Panthers' cleric, Father Earl A. Neil. A long-time member of the NAACP and the SCLC, Neil migrated from Chicago to the Bay Area in July 1967. He had heard about the Black Panthers in Chicago and related to their ten-point program. He believed that the "Black Panther Party [had] the most incisive analysis and response to the scene in America." During February 1968 he first visited the Alameda County jail to see Huey. Father Neil offered his church as a site where the Panthers could meet.

Soon police officers also targeted Father Neil. On April 3, 1968, armed police surrounded and entered his church, where Panthers were meeting. The police were accompanied by a white Catholic priest and a black clergyman. David Hilliard, the highest-ranking Panther at the meeting, refused to allow the police to enter the church's sanctuary. The following day, Father Neil held a press conference and denounced the police officers and the Oakland establishment. Undeterred by the outlaw behavior of the Oakland police, Father Neil allowed the Panthers to use his church for their Free Breakfast for Children Program.

Bobby Seale utilized his organizing skills and brilliantly launched the program by advertising as early as October 1968 in *The Black Panther* for supplies and volunteers to prepare and serve free breakfasts. The Party strategically wanted to include community members, grandmothers, and guardians. The FBCP provided a free, hot, nutritionally-balanced breakfast for school-age children. Panthers located facilities with kitchens big enough to feed large numbers with speed and efficiency. They had to have room for chairs and tables to seat at least 50. The Party tried to keep the names and addresses of the children it served. A minimum of ten individuals were assigned to each facility to control traffic, to help the children cross the street, to write down names, to be servers and table attendants and cooks. Some workers got up at 3:00 in the morning to arrive on time to feed the children. Local merchants were encouraged to donate food or money to the program. Because the FBCP operated from churches, the Party was able to secure a tax-free status as a nonprofit organization. Members were able to solicit donations and guarantee a tax exemption. In *The Black Panther* the FBCP advertisement included a statement of suggested foods and paper goods needed for donation on both one-time and long-term bases.

The FBCP caught on like wildfire and all forty-five chapters were instructed to set up the program. Panthers operated from the premise that "The youth they feed will feed the revolution." They were "liberating" children from hunger. On March 17, 1969, Vallejo, California Panthers started the FBCP with 35 children; within a week it grew to 110. The Chicago chapter reported on April 1, 1969, that they began with 83 children; by the end of the week they fed 1,100. The April 27, 1969, edition of *The Black Panther* reported on the success of the FBPC in northern California. More than 165 children at St. Augustine's Church were fed daily; St. Bernard's Church fed 100 children; San Francisco Sacred Heart fed 97; Douglas Rick fed 82; Hunter's Point fed 75; Richmond fed 110. Some chapters named their FBCP after fallen comrades. The Southern California chapter honored John Huggins. By the end of 1969, breakfasts were served by twenty-three chapters in nineteen cities. More than 20,000 children received a meal. Most of the programs were located in predominantly black communities, but the Panthers also fed children of other ethnic groups. One Seattle program operated in a predominantly poor white neighborhood.

Although the churches offered facilities, the Panthers were responsible for the supplies and food. At times Panthers were highly aggressive in securing food. In Seattle, Safeway stores received a letter signed by Panther breakfast coordinator Elmer Dixon. He requested

Previous page: **H**uey Newton addresses followers after his release on bail from prison, August 6, 1970.

Below: Newton, right, with Rev. Hazaiah Williams of the Center for Urban Black Theological Studies in May 1971.

Kansas City Panthers serve
free breakfasts to children
before they go to school.

$100 a week in food or funds for the breakfast program. In Seattle, smaller stores enthusiastically supported the FBCP. However, across the country Safeway stores located within the predominantly black community refused to donate food and seldomly employed African Americans. If the support was not received, a boycott would ensue. Safeway identified the behavior of some Panthers with extortion. Dixon and others throughout the nation were arrested and charged with extortion in their attempt to generate resources for the FBCP.

The Panthers made good on their threats to boycott businesses that did not give back to the community. The Oakland Safeway store was boycotted for refusal to donate needed food for the FBCP. In August 1971, Oakland Panthers also boycotted Bill Boyette, a black owner of several liquor stores and president of the Cal State Package Store and Taverns Owners' Association. Boyette solicited the Panthers' help when he was discriminated against by Mayfair stores. The Party was able to shut down Mayfair stores within four days. In return, Boyette promised to donate weekly supplies or funds to the FBCP. In the beginning Boyette met his part of the

Above: **A**t a rally in Jersey City, New Jersey, Panthers offer food to neighborhood youth.

Opposite and following pages: Free food programs run by the Black Panthers were in operation across the country.

agreement, but when he backslid the Panthers boycotted his liquor stores. Eventually the Panthers expanded this boycott to include other liquor stores that sold intoxicants to youths. Liquor stores owned by professional black entertainers and athletes were not able to escape the Panther picket lines.

Local police, in conjunction with the federal government, criticized the FBCP as a way to indoctrinate hate and violence into the children. Officers went into neighborhoods and told parents the Party was teaching racism and teaching children to riot at school. When the officers made their rounds, breakfast attendance would fall off. On August 8, 1969, Watts policemen terrorized children in a raid on a breakfast program. Five Panthers were arrested, but all charges were dropped.

Churches assisting the Panthers were harassed to deter them from continuing support. In San Diego, an FBI agent placed telephone calls and wrote anonymous letters to the auxiliary bishop of the Catholic diocese. His reports claimed that parishioners were upset about the priest's support of the breakfast program. The FBI reported in an internal memorandum that the priest had been "neutralized" and the program at that church ended.

Police also put pressure on store owners and individuals donating to the program. They would inquire about their finances and threaten IRS audits. Law enforcement agencies refused to admit that the program was nonviolent and of a humanitarian nature. In the past, police raids targeted Panthers and their guns, but now they included destroying food and supplies needed for the meals. Police would bust open pancake boxes, shoot water into the storage area and spread rumors that the food was poisoned. Almost every major city where Panthers hosted the FBCP reported food destroyed and donated money stolen by the police during unprovoked raids. Men paid to protect and serve the people were sabotaging a much-needed community program.

Other communities, such as the Mexican-American La Raza, began to adopt the Panther FBCP model. In 1978 under Title 42, Chapter 13A, an amendment was created to the Child Nutrition Act of 1966. It extended free lunch and breakfast to kids in households receiving assistance under the Food Stamp program or Aid to Families with Dependent Children. The federal government conceded it had to do more for children. A Panther program was folded into the national agenda.

Panthers expanded their FBCP to include free food for others in the community. The Party's food bank provided an ongoing supply of food when needed through periodic mass distributions at different locations throughout the community. Churches provided space to store perishable goods. Citizens donated the use of their cars for transportation, distributed flyers, solicited donations, and assisted in the actual distribution of the food. All citizens in need were given a minimum of a week's supply of food that included eggs, canned foods, vegetables, chicken, potatoes, rice, milk, etc. The Party believed that the food programs would spur the oppressed to end "the robbery [high prices for food] by the capitalists." They wanted the community to protest against the stores that exploited them. At times, community members joined their picket lines.

On occasion, the police harassed citizens who participated. In Oakland, John Siaz used his camper to pick up food and distribute *The Black Panther*. On February 22, 1970, his truck was firebombed. In Jersey City, New Jersey, a slumlord tried to evict a tenant for placing two Panther posters in her window.

Feeding the people was the first of many programs. In June 1969, the Oakland Panthers opened the first free medical health clinic in Berkeley. The Panthers believed that the federal government should provide universal health care. The Panthers were concerned with treating illnesses, "most of which are a result of oppression," along with developing preventive medical programs "to guarantee our future survival." They successfully solicited physicians, registered nurses, and medical students to donate time to their

clinics. Some local hospitals allowed doctors to use their laboratories for testing. Panthers knew that they could not exclusively rely on others to run their programs. Thus they incorporated in the Party's initiation process the formation of medical cadres. Panthers were trained in first aid and some were certified from accredited hospitals to give polio vaccinations, draw blood, conduct sickle cell anemia testing, etc. Unlike the FBCP, the health clinics required highly skilled workers and technical equipment. Thus, fewer chapters were able to implement this program. But they were also attacked. On July 5, 1970, the Boston clinic trailer was shot at thirteen times.

The Panthers brought national attention to sickle cell anemia, a disease that primarily impacts African American youth. By 1971 the Party created the Sickle Cell Anemia Research Foundation, a nation-wide program to test and to inform society about the disease. By 1974 Party members tested close to five hundred thousand people. Panthers also wrote proposals to secure funds for medical research, which the profession had severely neglected. The Party encouraged citizens to ask questions in hopes that they would organize to change existing health care services to serve the needs of the people better .

In Winston-Salem, North Carolina, Party members added a Free Ambulance Program to their medical agenda. Adequate ambulance

service was a problem in black communities across the country. Hospitals would refuse to send ambulances to certain communities or charge high prices. Panthers would transport individuals with a trained medical technician. The Party was able to secure the ambulance with a grant from the National Episcopal Church General Convention Special Program.

Panthers addressed the high rates of unemployment in the community by creating a Free Employment Program and Job Information Network. They set up an office, went into the community looking for jobs, and encouraged owners to create jobs when possible. Panthers obtained job listings from state and local government agencies and gave tips on how to maintain contact with a prospective employer. They believed that "everyone has the right to a job, not only to guarantee survival, but to give a decent standard of living."

Party members also responded to requests by seniors for protection against muggings, especially when they went to cash their Social Security and pension checks. Seniors had gone to the Oakland police department for assistance, but their complaints fell on deaf ears. Officers simply told the citizens to walk close to the curb. The Party organized the Seniors Against a Fearful Environment Program (SAFE). In a 1974 funding proposal, the Party documented

Opposite: **H**uey Newton visits the People's Republic of China in 1971, where he meets with Premier Zhou Enlai.

Below: Panther children and teenagers outside their Liberation School in the Fillmore district of San Fransisco

that over a six-week period beginning in late August 1972, of the 249 victims of robbery, 48 percent were over age 50. Overall 33 percent of all crimes in Oakland in 1972 were committed against seniors. S.A.F.E. offered free transportation and escort services for seniors at the beginning of each month.

Black Panthers also created Free Shoes and Clothing programs by asking shoe factories to donate shoes that were in storage because they were outdated models. These donations could be written off as charitable contributions. After David Hilliard was incarcerated, the shoe program was renamed the David Hilliard Free Shoe Program. The Free Clothing Program solicited major department stores to reduce their prices. At times, some stores gave the Party free clothing. Together these programs fulfilled the Party's desire to work with community members and become unified in their efforts to demand more from the state and federal governments.

Though chapters received instructions from national headquarters on the implementation of survival programs, they also gave the local chapters room to create programs to address their communities' specific needs. In Dallas, Panthers organized a free pest control service for hundreds of public housing residents to exterminate roaches and rats. Party members secured funds and supplies from black-owned businesses, churches, and social clubs.

In 1970 the Southern California chapter provided a Legal Aid for Prisoners Program and ran free bus transportation to jails and prisons for family members. By 1972 they were able to purchase a 40-passenger bus, which made weekly trips to a variety of incarceration facilities. A schedule was circulated throughout the community. The Party provided free food for the citizens while riding the bus and ran a Free Commissary for Prisoners Program. The Party contended that prisoners had the right to live and function as human beings. Denial of basic "privileges" to "bathe, to have warm and adequate clothing, legal books and other reading material" was wrong.

Many Panthers lived in a communal environment. Often children did not live with their biological parents but stayed in a safe-house environment created by the Party. Women and men successfully shared childcare responsibility. It is not surprising that Panthers continued to initiate programs targeted toward youth. The FBCP fed children during the school year, but what about the summer months? Panthers organized liberation summer schools beginning on June 25, 1969, in San Francisco. The schools fulfilled the Party demand for education for people that "exposes the true nature of this decadent American society" and teaches "our true history and our role in the present-day society." Children (ages 2 to 13) began their day with breakfast, and their weekly curriculum was as follows:

Mon: Revolutionary History Day
Tue: Revolutionary Culture Day
Wed: Current Event Day
Thur: Movie Day
Fri: Field Trip Day

During the evening liberation schools were transformed into political education classes for adults and dinner was offered.

Right: **S**tudents at a liberation summer school.

Other survival programs included: petitions for community control of police; voter registration drive; community news reporters; legal aid and advice; community pig watch; student action committee.

Chapters submitted weekly reports to national headquarters documenting their program activities, which were then printed in *The Black Panther*. Of course, the size of the chapter and its resources determined the ability to carry out programs. While the activism of women was always crucial, their labor fueled the program's success. The Panthers combined the rhetoric of revolution with a bona fide social agenda. Without a doubt the Panther programs served the community, and in turn the people sustained the Party.

With Huey Newton incarcerated and Eldridge Cleaver in exile, the programs were under the leadership of Bobby Seale and David Hilliard. The Central Committee agreed that the success of the survival programs depended on the strength of the Party. The committee decided to accelerate the attrition of Panthers. "Jackanapes" had to be removed. Seale explained that a jackanape "is a fool. He's foolish, but he's not scared of the police. He's foolish in that he'll get himself killed quicker. If you don't straighten him out, and try to politically educate him, he will definitely bring the Party down." "Jackanapes" described Panthers who strayed and violated basic rules of the Party. By early 1969 the Central Committee expanded the Party's rules from ten to twenty-six. Seale wrote that some of the additional rules were geared toward specific individuals. The Central Committee elected to clamp down on destructive behavior. Bobby and David refused to bail out members arrested for possession of marijuana, riding in cars with no registrations, carrying guns without the authority of the Central Committee, etc. Internal dissensions increased as longtime Panthers found themselves denied bail while others favored by the leadership had access to the organizations treasury. The Central Committee decided to purge the ranks of jackanapes, informers, and agents provocateurs.

Panthers had been expelled in the past, but beginning in January 1969, large numbers were ousted. Alleged jackanapes were expelled in far greater number than certified informers. The Central Committee published the names of purged members in *The Black Panther* with reasons why they were expelled. During the second main purge between March and August 1969, more than 250 Panthers were listed expelled: 38 were tagged "reactionary," 62 were "renegades," 24 were "counterrevolutionary," 17 were accused of trying to "take over the Boston" chapter, 8 were identified as "informer of FBI or police," and 60 Panthers were expelled without explanation. The remainder were purged on charges that ranged from "jive nigger" to "desire to leave." The chapters that were hit hardest were East Oakland; Vallejo, California; Boston; Jersey City; and New York City.

There is no question that some of the expelled members engaged in reckless behavior. However, many were dedicated freedom fighters who either questioned the direction of Party leadership, were misrepresented by others, or refused to be silent in the midst of chaos. The fact that someone could be expelled as a "jive nigger" substantiates the notion that some of the decisions by the Central Committee were not based on concrete evidence. The Party man-

Below: **P**anther demonstrators on January 6, 1970 outside the Los Angeles Hall of Justice during a hearing for Panthers arrested during the police shootout.

aged to purge itself while simultaneously initiating survival programs throughout the country.

The Party was stunned when police kidnapped Bobby Seale on August 19, 1969, as he left the wedding of Panthers Masia Hewitt and Shirley Neely. Seale was implicated in the brutal murder of Panther Alex Rackley, alleged to be a police informer, in New Haven, Connecticut. The following day he was released on bail, rearrested, and charged with inciting a riot at the 1968 Democratic National Convention in Chicago. Seale's two major cases would keep him incarcerated for a lengthy period. By default David Hilliard became the leader of the Party.

Hilliard cultivated special relationships with some members, including Elmer "Geromino" Pratt from the Southern California chapter. By and large, he surrounded himself with trusted family members. His brother June became assistant chief of staff, and his wife, Patricia, the financial secretary. According to Patricia:

> *I had always been a bookkeeper and cashier so I also took care of the money. I couldn't have anything on paper because they had started breaking into offices, killing Panthers. I had a little tablet and my own codes for six running accounts in my head: two bank accounts for the newspaper, the Huey P. Newton Defense*

Above: **B**obby Seale addresses the opening session of the Party's national conference in July, 1969.

Fund, the Black Panther Party fund, a bail fund, and one more. I did no business over the phone. If they started talking business, I'd take the conversation somewhere else.

The siblings of Huey and Bobby continued to remain closely tied to the Central Committee. However, the gap between the rank-and-file membership and the Central Committee was widening. Many complained about the allocation of Party funds. While Hilliard was loyal and committed to the Party, he lacked the skills to fairly resolve conflict. As the main spokesperson for the Party, Hilliard was forced to represent the organization. Hilliard's memoir reveals that unlike Cleaver or Seale, he was not comfortable in the limelight. Fred Hampton suggested that he not be "so controlled" and to get "emotional" when he spoke on behalf of the Party. At a November 15, 1969, antiwar rally, even though he was coached on what to say, once he reached the podium, he deviated from the script.

I'm never gonna stop cursing.... Not only are we going to curse, we're gonna put into practice some of the shit we talk about. Because Richard Nixon is an evil man. This is the motherfucker that unleashed the counterinsurgent teams upon the Black Panther Party. This is the man that's responsible for all the attacks on the Black Panther Party nationally. This is the man that sends his vicious murderous dogs out into the black community and invades our Black Panther Party breakfast programs. Destroys food that we have for hungry kids and expects us to accept shit like that

idly....Fuck that motherfucking man!....We will kill Richard Nixon.

Hilliard's speech was interpreted by the government as a direct threat against President Nixon. In 1970 Nixon and Hoover declared that the destruction of the Black Panther Party was a "national priority." Two weeks later Hilliard was arrested and bail was set at fifty thousand dollars. During his incarceration, Fred Hampton and Mark Clark were killed, and the Los Angeles chapter was ambushed by the police department. After bail was posted, large amounts of unsolicited money rolled into the Party for the New York 21 defense and other pending Panther cases. The New York 21 aggressively spoke out against the system. On April 12, 1970 the Panther 21 defense office and legal papers were burned. The FBI was on the scene before the fire department arrived. One lawyer allowed in the office reported that some of the files appeared to have been deliberately burned. Panther Dharuba wrote, "The N.Y. 21 must be set free or the pigs oink will become the language of mankind, and there will be no warriors who will stand

Opposite top: **F**BI director J. Edgar Hoover, left, and President Richard Nixon in 1971.

Opposite bottom: **Photograph released by Oakland and Berkeley police, who claimed the guns and ammunition were seized at the Black Panther headquarters in April 1974**

Above: **Demonstrators supporting the twenty-one Panthers on trial in New York.**

between the people and the pigs to ensure our liberation." On May 31, 1971, the New York 21 were unanimously acquitted. Hilliard bounced from California to Chicago to New Haven and New York in efforts to secure the release of incarcerated Panthers.

He and other Panthers were also battling FBI attacks. By the end of 1969, COINTEL-PRO made 233 separate Panther raids. Offices were still a main target, and when the Party renamed their offices the National Committee to Combat Fascism Community Information Center (NCCF) in July 1970, attacks increased. In Cleveland on July 4, 1970, more than 100 police carried out a military assault on the NCCF office. In August 1970, at 6:00 A.M., Philadelphia's tactical squads and the FBI raided three Party offices. They axed down doors and teargassed occupants at one location. At another office the police made the fifteen male and female Panthers strip naked and then began shooting at them.

Above: **P**anthers and cops on the march in New York City.

Below: Panther Wayne Pharr and a friend leave the Los Angeles Hall of Justice after Pharr and eleven other Panthers are acquitted of most of the charges brought against them after the 1969 police assault on Panther headquarters.

Finally, on August 5, 1970, Huey P. Newton was released from prison on fifty thousand dollars bail pending a new trial. The rank-and-file members, many of whom had never met Newton, expected much from him. Newton reflected that "although people received me warmly, I was at first a symbol. Our relationship had changed. There was now an element of hero worship that had not existed before I

got busted." Huey wrote that he simply wanted to relate to the brothers and sisters on the block in a low-key fashion, but comrades close to him sensed that Huey felt left out and wanted deference. David changed Huey's Party title from minister of defense to supreme servant. This was the beginning of many problems with Huey.

Huey had to prepare for the Constitutional Convention arranged by Eldridge Cleaver, who proposed two Revolutionary Constitutional Convention meetings to rewrite the Constitution of the United States, the first in September 1970. Newton was apprehensive about these conventions because they had no power for implementation, but he went along with the Party's decision. Eldridge guaranteed that Kathleen, who had great drawing power, would return from Algeria and speak at the second convention scheduled to take place Thanksgiving weekend. At the first convention, comrades were sorely disappointed with Newton's convoluted, philosophical speech. On the eve of the second convention, the legend contends, Eldridge decided not to let Kathleen return to the United States. Huey viewed this poorly planned convention as a major setback. The Party received many negative letters when they were unable to write a new constitution to "overthrow the government by force."

Without a doubt, COINTELPRO agents compounded the communication problems between Cleaver and Newton. The FBI continued to monitor Eldridge in Algiers. It sent a stream of letters to

Previous page: **N**ewton, with Robert Bay, leaves the Alameda County Court House in Oakland in December 1971 after dismissal of a manslaughter charge against him.

Below: Headquarters of the international section of the Black Panthers in Algiers.

Cleaver stating that the Party leaders in California were seeking to undercut his influence. Newton was perturbed by Cleaver's far-reaching impact on Party members. Hilliard recalled that Newton complained, "Everybody acts like Eldridge. The profanity. Eldridge's style. Eldridge has taken you guys down his direction. This isn't the way of the Party." Many say that Newton was paranoid and easily agitated after his release. Anything, including shock treatment, could have happened to him in prison. COINTELPRO's illegal activities to neutralize the Party only enhanced Huey's suspicions. His comrades said that he zeroed in on particular members for no apparent reasons. Hilliard could not understand why Huey refused to embrace Geronimo Pratt, whom Huey accused of being too militaristic. Geronimo stated in *The Black Panther* of January 10, 1970, that "all the nickel and dime games that you play on the oppressed people must stop. All the red devils, trues, and drugs must go. Those El Dorados will have to turn into tanks, and those bad rags, into gun and ammo." Newton dismissed Pratt's suggestions at Central Committee meetings and finally accused him of being an agent. To remove Newton's suspicions in June 1970, Pratt took a battery of loyalty tests. After he passed them, Huey argued that he had learned manipulative skills in the military. Newton instructed Hilliard to write the statement on Geromino's expulsion, which Hilliard refused to do. Newton then had Elaine Brown, a Southern California Panther, now a member of the Central Committee, write the letter. On January 23, 1971, Newton published in *The Black Panther* that Geronimo and Sandra (Red) Pratt, along with other Los Angeles Panthers, were expelled. In 1968, Pratt had been accused of killing a teacher in Santa Monica. He had been incarcerated since June 23, 1969, and held without bond. His expulsion effectively isolated him from Party defense funds.

In February 1971, Newton appeared on Jim Dunbar's call-in talk show based in San Francisco. Newton arranged to have Cleaver connected via telephone from Algiers. Cleaver criticized the Central Committee's decision to expel Pratt and other "Cleaverite" members of the Party and launched an aggressive attack against David Hilliard. After Cleaver's statements, key members in four branches in New York and New Jersey resigned from the Party in support of Eldridge, and other members left altogether. The Party was characterized by many as now split into two factions: East Coast, West Coast. But it was not that cut and dried.

Newton expelled the entire international wing of the Party. On March 5, 1971, Cleaver in turn expelled Huey Newton and David Hilliard.

The Cleaver-Newton split drastically impacted the Pratts. In November 1971, Geromino's wife Sandra, eight months pregnant, was shot five times at point-blank range. Her body was then stuffed in a sleeping bag and dumped on the side of a Los Angeles freeway. Mysteriously, no one was ever charged with the murder. By June 1972, Pratt's trial for the 1968 murder of a teacher on a Santa Monica tennis court began. With no access to Party funds Pratt had to rely on a court-appointed attorney, an inexperienced Johnnie Cochran. At the time of the murder Pratt was four hundred miles

Above: **G**eronimo Pratt, whom Newton expelled from the party. Pratt remains in prison on bogus charges.

Below: **E**laine Brown, a party leader, and at bottom, Erica Huggins, one of the leaders of the Oakland Intercommunal Youth institute.

Opposite: Children at the Oakland Intercommunal Youth Institute.

away in Oakland, attending a Party Central Committee meeting. Because of the factionalism, all of Newton's supporters in attendance (including David, June and Pat Hilliard, Bobby and John Seale, Nathan Hare, Rosemary Gross, and Brenda Presley) refused to testify on behalf of Pratt. Kathleen Cleaver had testified that Pratt was indeed at the meeting, but COINTELPRO letters to Eldridge explained that it was "too dangerous" for Kathleen to return to the United States for the trial. Pratt was convicted in 1972. He has been in prison for twenty-three years. Johnnie Cochran, later to become famous as O.J. Simpson's attorney, stated he cannot "forget or forgive" Geronimo Pratt's case. After Cochran took the case he also became a target of the government. "They had wiretapped my phone; they had informants around us who was working with us for the FBI; they had informants who lied in court....If the government wants to get you, they will," Cochran concluded that he will not quit practicing law until Pratt is out of prison.

After the Cleaver-Newton split, Huey moved the Party to a more ideological plane. He had always been a philosopher and keenly interested in theoretical ideas. Many now felt that the Party had become deradicalized. To some the Panther programs resembled reform units. Elaine Brown became a major spokesperson for the Party during this period of flux. She recalled that Huey responded to this criticism by saying, "This is my party, and we'll have breakfast, lunch, and dinner programs if I say so. And I do..." How could one have a revolution without guns? Brown wrote that Mao said, "In order to get rid of the gun it is necessary to take up the gun. And we believe that. But we have to emphasize that the idea is to get rid of the gun."

When Newton took residence in a penthouse off Lake Merritt across the way from the Alameda County Court house in Oakland, comrades were taken aback. Why wasn't Huey living among the people? Elaine Brown explained that after Huey was released from prison he had no place to stay. He would go from one comrade's house to another, and they were concerned about his safety. They located the penthouse apartment for $650 per month. Elaine solicited enough money from a "Hollywood donor" to pay the rent for an entire year. Before the Central Committee could explain to the rank-and-file members why Huey was living away from them, the FBI leaked the story to the *San Francisco Examiner.* The penthouse became a major point of discussion for the members. It was too expensive and unlike the majority of other Panther homes, which were shared in common, it was Newton's domain.

Newton continued to support and expand the Panther programs but renamed them "survival programs pending revolution." The addition of a Child Development Center, a 24-hour child-care facility for children between ages of 2 months and 3 years, was welcomed by the Oakland community. By May 19, 1970, thirty chapters implemented the Party's survival programs. Huey attempted to pull Panthers from other states to Oakland to centralize the Party's efforts. He thought the Party should use Oakland as a model to prove to the world what could happen when black citizenry united in a local community. Some members complied; others were committed to stay in the communities they initially had pledged to serve.

After Newton and Yale University philosopher Erik Erikson jointly presented a week-long seminar in early 1971, Huey decided that he wanted to open a more sophisticated school than the summer liberation school. He wanted to rescue "the comrades from their ideological stagnation"; he wanted them to learn "how to think," not "what to think." Elaine Brown reasoned that the ideological institute would be a way for Huey to reaffirm his place in the Party. While many Panthers left the Party because it no longer resembled the organization they originally joined, new recruits adopted the Party's new agenda.

A stepping-stone to Newton's Ideological Institute was the establishment of the Intercommunal Youth Institute in Oakland in January 1971. The Institute was in direct response to the poor public school system that did not teach children how to think in an analytical way. The March 27, 1971, edition of *The Black Panther* reported that there were twenty-eight children enrolled. They lived at the Institute during the week and returned home on the weekends. Under the leadership of Brenda Bay and Erica Huggins, the school blossomed. In October 1973, the Institute moved to a larger location and was renamed the Oakland Community Learning Center. By 1974 more than one hundred Panther and community children between ages of 2 and 11 were enrolled. The staff of nineteen taught a diverse curriculum of math, language arts, science, art, health, and political education, which also included Mexican-American history and environmental studies. When the children graduated from the institute they were advanced in their studies. Some were even skipped in junior high and sent directly to high school. The money earned from the Party's lease of a movie theater paid for the Institute. By 1974, the Party created a booklet describing all the programs in detail, with directions on their implementation.

The FBI continued to be perturbed by the Panthers' commitment to build community institutions. Their constant surveillance and jailing of Panthers kept them under siege. Increased use of heavy drugs aided in the Party's destruction. As early as November 1969, *The Black Panther* warned schoolchildren about drugs sold on playgrounds. A May 9, 1970 article by Panther Michael Tabor, "Capitalism Plus Dope Equals Genocide," discussed drug addiction as a "monstrous symptom of the malignancy which is ravaging the social fabric of the capitalist system." In October 1970, a Philadelphia Panther observed a policeman giving a nine-year-old girl a heroin-soaked sugar cube in the Richard Allen Project. Panthers cautioned children not to accept candy from anyone. On December 31, 1971, the "H. Rap Brown Antidope Movement" was launched. Brown was charged with attempted murder and robbery when he attempted to shut down a "dope spot." By this period, drug abuse had reached epidemic proportions in black communities.

While drinking and smoking marijuana were acceptable "off duty," dope was prohibited. Junkies were not allowed in the Party office. In fact, psychedelic drugs were seen as counterrevolutionary because they were destructive to the body. But Panthers did not live in a vacuum. Some increased their use of highly expensive cocaine as they mingled with Hollywood celebrities. Once the Party purchased the Lamp Post nightclub, drugs were very present. Huey Newton's addiction to cocaine and alcohol induced him to behave recklessly. More and more comrades came to mimic his gangster-like behavior. Dr. Tolbert Smalls recalled that when he began working at the party's health clinic the cadre were reading Chairman Mao's *Quotations*. "By the time I left the Party, I'd come in and the same cadre would be reading *The Godfather*."

By 1974, Elaine complained to Huey that drugs were rampant. Cocaine could be purchased cheaply. "It's coming into Oakland at low prices from I don't know where….Young niggers—sixteen and seventeen years old—were perched on the rooftops with automatic rifles…." protecting their drug territory. Drugs permeated the black community. After Seale was acquitted on both the Chicago and New Haven charges in June 1971, he once again joined his friend and comrade Huey Newton. Their relationship had changed, primarily because Huey was on drugs and was paranoid. But Seale hung with the Party and Newton's decisions—no matter how chaotic.

On August 21, 1971, Newton, Seale, and the entire Black Panther

Opposite top: **G**eorge Jackson's mother, Georgia, surrounded by Panthers as they object to photographs taken at George's burial service in Mt. Vernon, Illinois.

Opposite below: Georgia Jackson.

Party were saddened by the assassination of Panther George Jackson. When Jackson was eighteen years old he had robbed a gas station of $70. He had served ten years of a one-year-to-life sentence. On January 13, 1970, a guard killed three black inmates at California's Soledad Prison. In retaliation a guard was killed. Jackson, Fleeta Drumgo, and John Cluchette were charged with the murder. Their case became known as that of the Soledad Brothers. Jonathan Jackson, George's younger brother, led the protest against the frame-up. On August 7, 1970, Jonathan attempted to free his brother. At a Marin County court, Jonathan armed three prisoners and took hostage a judge, district attorney, and three jurors. In the end four people were killed, including Jonathan, two inmates, and the judge. Professor Angela Davis immediately became the FBI's target because she was head of the Soledad Brothers' Defense Committee. Two of the guns used in the shoot-out were legally registered to Davis, who became the FBI's "most wanted fugitive." She was captured in October 1970.

In prison, Jackson had become a revolutionary and wrote for *The Black Panther*. His book *Soledad Brother* was published nationwide in a mass-market paperback edition. It articulated his brilliant

Top: **A**ngela Davis speaking against the death penalty in North Carolina, July 1974.

Below: Davis giving the black power salute in a San Rafael, California courtroom.

Opposite: A birthday party at the Huey P. Newton Youth Institute in February 1973. Posters support Bobby Seale's campaign for mayor of Oakland and Elaine Brown's for councilwoman.

vision of the need to empower the oppressed, especially prisoners who are the victims of social injustice. Jackson had organized San Quentin inmates into a branch of the Party in 1971. His incarceration made him a sitting duck for the FBI. The notorious agent Louis Tackwood was assigned the mission to kill Jackson. Tackwood orchestrated a possible escape, and during the melee Jackson was gunned down. Jackson's funeral in Oakland was reminiscent of Lil' Bobby Hutton's. George Jackson was one of the few people Huey respected and admired, and his murder devastated him. Patricia Hilliard confirmed the change in Huey. "I think George's death brought home to him that he wasn't invincible. But after that he just became very suspicious…suspicious of everybody. His cousins, his relatives, his brother." The Party attempted to regroup after Jackson's funeral, but it was difficult. Death was omnipresent, and long-time members were tired of going to funerals. How could the Party not pick up the guns? How could they not defend themselves? A dialectical struggle developed between members on the direction of the Party. When Huey was freed on December 15, 1971, after his third mistrial, and was acquitted of all charges connected to the Frey shoot-out, some believed he would be the "old Huey."

On March 29, 1972, Newton altered the Black Panther Party's ten-point program:

Point No. 6: "We want all black men to be exempt from the military service" was changed to "We want completely free health care for all black and oppressed people."

Point No. 7: "We want an immediate end to police brutality and murder of black people" was changed to "We want an immediate end to police brutality and murder of black people, other people of color, all oppressed people inside the United States."

Point No. 8: "We want freedom for all black men held in federal, state, county, and city prisons and jails" was changed to "We want an immediate end to all wars of aggression."

Point No. 9: "We want all black people when brought to trial to be tried by a jury of their peer group or people from their black communities as defined by the Constitution of the United States" was changed to "We want freedom for all black and oppressed people now held in U.S. Federal, State, County, City, and military prisons and jails. We want trials by a jury of peers for all persons charged with so-called crimes under the laws of this country."

Point No. 10: "We want land, bread, housing, education, clothing justice and peace" was changed to "We want land, bread, housing, education, clothing, justice, peace, and people's community control of modern technology."

Newton decided that Bobby Seale should run for mayor of Oakland and Elaine Brown for City Council in the April 1973 election. Panthers pooled their resources in a full-fledged campaign to get their candidates elected. Seale utilized his legendary organizational skills and announced their candidacies at one of the mass Free Food programs. They shed their leather jackets and berets and campaigned in a serious attempt to garner votes while attacking Oakland's institutions. Elaine complained that she was often frustrated

Below: **B**obby Seale campaigns for mayor of Oakland, with Elaine Brown, running for Oakland City Council, April 1973.

Opposite top: Kathleen Cleaver at an August 1972 news conference in San Francisco. She accused the CIA of trying to assassinate her husband who was self-exiled in Algeria.

Opposite bottom: Huey Newton, right, chatting with his attorney, Michael Kennedy, in 1979. Newton was charged with slaying a young woman in 1974

with Bobby's clowning. She feared it made their race a sideshow. In reality, Bobby's personality and ability to connect with the people strengthened their candidacy. Neither Seale nor Brown won. However, the black community overwhelmingly supported them. Elaine lost by 4,000 votes. Seale was in a seven-way race, and his votes put him in a runoff with Republican John Reading, who won the election with 77,634 votes. Seale received 43,719 and won 158 precincts. Reading spent $163,988 for his campaigned compared to Seale's $67,170. The Panthers were proud of their accomplishment, and Seale refused to make a concession speech. "They like people to make concession speeches. I don't make concession speeches. I will not concede the rights—the human rights—of human beings."

This was one of the last major Party activities for Seale. Huey was out of control and surrounded himself with yes-men and yes-women. Newton took it upon himself to expel David Hilliard, who was still in jail after his Nixon statement. Huey had received bogus FBI letters warning him that others believed David was a stronger leader than he. When Masai Hewitt complained about the Central Committee not being a democratic body, Huey reduced him to sell-

ing the newspaper and then arranged for him to be beaten. On one of his cocaine and alcohol binges, Huey cursed Seale and told him he was no longer a Panther. Two days later, Huey bestowed the chairman title on Elaine Brown. By this time, the Black Panther Party was no longer a functioning national organization.

Elaine Brown did her best to keep the Party afloat. She placed more women in influential Party positions. Erica Huggins was elected to the Alameda County Board of Education, the highest elected post won by a Panther. Committed members kept the survival programs going, and their school had a waiting list. By the summer of 1974, Huey's destructiveness caught up with him. He had pistol-whipped a tailor, Preston Collins, and was charged with the murder of a teenager, Kathleen Smith. In August, Huey and his girlfriend Gwen fled to Cuba. Brown was left in complete charge of the deteriorating Party. She knew she had to command the respect of the rank and file. She opted to use Newton's manipulative style and rule with an iron hand: "I have all the guns and all the money. I can withstand challenge from without and from within." Brown surrounded herself with bodyguards and, though a victim of beatings

Below: **E**ldridge Cleaver in 1987.

Bottom: **Bobby Seale in 1994.**

Opposite: **Huey Newton and wife Gwen after five-year-old murder charges against him were dropped in September 1979.**

herself, at times she tragically replicated slavemaster tactics on others. "Some men were beaten by my hand—or authority—as were some women," she aknowledged in a 1993 essay in the *New York Times.* She worked within the system to gain community control and became a member of the Oakland Council for Economic Development, which was composed of sixteen top business and industries concerned with city economic development. Brown successfully lobbied for jobs and was instrumental in the election of Lionel Wilson for mayor. Under her leadership the Party became a stronger political voice in Oakland, but she was unable to make the Party a significant national organization.

When Cleaver returned from exile in 1975, he was a different man. The Revolutionary Student Brigade wrote, "...Cleaver crawled back from exile a traitor to the struggle of black people, and the struggles of all people for liberation."

Cleaver became a born-again Christian, and the *Reader's Digest* quoted him saying: "I'd rather be in jail in America than free anywhere else." On August 13, 1976, Arthur DeMoss, a wealthy Christian businessman, provided most of the collateral to free Cleaver on his $100,000 bail. After his release, Cleaver prayed with Pat Boone, Billy Graham, and other newsworthy white Christians.

Kathleen Cleaver also matured during their time in Algeria and Paris. "I'm older and wiser. I've lost my romanticism about revolution in America. I don't say it's inconceivable, but I know that none of us who believed ourselves to be revolutionaries in the 1960s can conceive of the form a revolution would take in America." When asked about the Black Panther Party she responded, "I don't know any people who claim to be members of the Black Panther Party. I don't know them; I don't know who they are."

Kathleen and Eldridge returned to the United States during the time when revolutionary political action was on the wane. Much of the left, Students for Democratic Society, and the PFP had splintered, Vietnam was no longer a rallying issue, middle-class youth who were a part of SNCC had graduated from college and were positioned to take advantage of the minimal civil rights gains. America had changed, and revolutionaries were no longer in vogue.

In 1977, Huey returned from Cuba to face murder charges. Elaine continued the Party's focus on local electoral politics. Newton entered a Ph.D. program in the history of consciousness at the University of California, Santa Cruz. Panther survival programs were fewer in number and plagued by financial trouble. The FBI kept fiscal records of the Party's main bank account. Their records reveal that on April 29, 1968, the national headquarters opened with a deposit of $710.50. As of October 1970, total deposits were $171,943.24, disbursements $172,302.96, overdrawn $359.72. A great majority of the money came from *The Black Panther.* By September 1970, the IRS began to hound the Party about its tax-exempt status. The Party contended that the organization was a political body similar to the Democrats or Republicans. In response, the Committee on Internal Security of the House of Representatives in 1969–1970 held a series of hearings about the Party. The Activist Organization Committee, also known as the Special Service (SS) group, identified the Party and twenty-two other organi-

zations to be investigated to determine "the sources of their funds, the names of...contributors, whether the contributions given...have been deducted as charitable contributions, [and] what it [i.e. IRS] can find out generally about the funds of these organizations."

By 1974 the IRS issued summonses to the Bank of America for all the Party records and audited Party leaders and contributors. Donations no longer even trickled into the organization. In 1982 the last survival program, the Youth Institute, closed its doors for lack of finances. Huey Newton was accused of embezzling the school funds.

In 1980 Newton earned his doctorate degree but drugs continued to rule his life. By 1987 he was incarcerated for possession of cocaine. On August 22, 1989, he was killed in West Oakland by a drug dealer. More than ten-thousand mourned his death at Oakland's Allen Temple Baptist Church. Though Huey's life ended in moral decay, he contributed much to the struggle for freedom and left a fierce legacy to the black liberation movement.

Newton was not the only Panther who became addicted to drugs and alcohol. The drugs medicated the pain of the Party's failure to survive, the pain of other Party and family members murdered, the pain caused by continual repression. In the beginning the Party members persecuted drug dealers; toward the end, too many of them became their clients. Its no wonder that many Panthers say they did not leave the Party, the Party left them.

Panthers fought a domestic war, and some still experience post-traumatic stress. Many of the rank-and-file members are nameless in the history books, but their courageous commitment as freedom fighters should never be forgotten or dismissed because of reckless behavior by some members. The symptoms that spurred the formation of the Black Panther Party are still ever present. Police brutality, high unemployment, homelessness, poor education, lack of universal health care—all still plague the nation. Drug addiction, particularly the flood of crack cocaine, has numbed an entire generation of Americans. Some former Panthers are still committed to the principles of the Party. No longer clad in their black leather jackets and berets, they still work on behalf of their communities in a variety of ways. African Americans have always fought against injustices, from slavery to the present. There always will be Black Panthers!

PART 2—THE FILM
MARIO VAN PEEBLES

GENESIS

This isn't just a novel man, this is a feature."

"Yeah," Pops grunted. "A feature Hollywood's never gonna make less they homogenize it first." He reclined in his seat, his limp half-chewed stogie balanced precariously on his lower lip, and closed his eyes.

"Later for Hollywood, we could finance it independently, circumvent the system, guerrilla film it."

In retrospect I'm not sure what all this "We" stuff was about. That was almost nine years ago and the "Me" half of the "We" didn't have the juice to get a job directing traffic, much less a feature film.

My dad and I had boarded the train in Philly, City of Brotherly Love, and we wouldn't be arriving in New York for another couple hours. The old man had used this ride as an opportunity to read me a chapter of his new novel on the TS (Top Secret)— that's what he'd classify any material deemed politically significant before he gave you a verbal taste. The novel, which was mostly scribbled longhand on yellow pieces of mismatched paper, was based on the rise of the Black Panther Party.

The Panthers believed that "the spirit of the people was greater than the man's technology." The story's premise was that the Panthers, knowing they would be infiltrated by the FBI and recognizing that their greatest resource was the human resource, picked certain loyal members to be double agents. The protagonist finds himself between the proverbial rock and a hard place, with the FBI on one front and the Panthers on the other, and through his eyes we're exposed to the inner workings of both.

Dad, in one of his revolutionary incarnations, had gotten pretty close to some of the Panthers, or so he'd have you believe. You never really know when Melvin Van Movies, political theorist, ex-Air Force astronomer, director-producer, Wall Street tycoon, singer, hustler, and writer happens also to be your father. At any rate, what he had read me was original, edgy, politically challenging, and it

moved. In short, I'd drink muddy water for a chance to direct it. But like I said, I couldn't have gotten a job directing much of anything at the time. And as far as having the weight as an actor to get Hollywood independents or otherwise to develop anything for me—zero, forget it. I was lucky to develop myself into anything beyond extra work. So what was all this let's-do-this-one-ourselves "We" stuff I was riffing? I suppose it's what the folks in L.A. call "positive visualization" or "projection" or what we call "talking stuff." There's still a certain amount of talking stuff when Pop and I get together. It seems to keep us warm, like two cats speculating on how they're going to spend their cash when they hit Lotto.

But whatever the reason, nine years after that train ride, we somehow got our shot. He wrote the script. I got to direct. And together we produced *Panther*.

Page 130: **T**he Van Peebles Boys—Mario, left, and Melvin.

Top left: **Wesley Jonathan as Lil' Bobby Hutton.**

Lower left: **Location filming of the Denzil Dowell rally.**

This page: **Tiny checks out Bernadette at the opening of the movie.**

ERACISM

The Black Panther Party for Self-Defense was sold to a relatively naive America as little more than a paramilitary group of gun-toting black militants, in short, neo-niggaz. The media told America about their arms but not about their food and breakfast programs for hungry youth. We heard more about their standing up to the police than we did about their free shoe giveaways, sickle cell anemia testing, schools, and even political campaigns. In spite of the fact that the Panthers were antioppression, they were portrayed as antiwhite. Chairman Bobby Seale said repeatedly, "We're not antiwhite, we're antioppression. We're not anti any race; we're antiracism."

The Panthers were inspired by political groups of almost all races and nationalities, from Che, Mao Zedong, Marx, Frantz Fanon, and Malcolm X to even the French underground. They were so impressed by the French Resistance that stood up against the German occupying army during World War II that they adopted the black French beret as part of their Panther uniform. Undoubtedly, if I had done a film about the French resisting Nazi oppression, race would have been a non-issue, because in this instance the oppressor and the oppressed were both Caucasian. But when the Black Panthers stood up to an oppressive police force and government that was largely white, their act of resistance was deliberately portrayed by the authorities as being antiwhite. Ironically, the victims of racism by resisting victimization were accused of being racist. Like the movement itself, any film about the Panthers' struggle against oppression runs the risk of being oversimplified as just a racial struggle.

Early on, when my dad and I were pitching the Panther story to various studios, we ran into the expected "color" resistance. One executive said he loved Huey, loved Bobby, loved everybody, and even loved the script with one exception. "Couldn't we make one of the lead Panthers white so the mainstream audience would feel more comfortable?" There was a long pause. I glanced at Dad to let him know that I'd field this question, because his response might have been less diplomatic.

I explained to the man that there were no white Panthers per se in the Black

Medium being part of the message, I felt the film's visual signature should reflect its "Empowerment —Power to the People" message. The film would start out small, intimate, almost a funky ghetto cinema verite. And as the Party grew, spreading out from Oakland into a national movement, the scope of the picture would grow as well. Eddie Pei, the director of photography, and I would let the camera ride with the story's own human dynamic. People would motivate camera moves, not vice versa, and as the revolutionaries became the revolution, we would photograph it with bigger, lyrical epic camera moves. The film's look should not have an ego; we didn't want anyone saying "that was a dope director's shot." Any sexy camera moves or transitions should not call attention to themselves, but rather be noticed subliminally, if at all, and only enhance the storytelling. Style should reflect content, not overshadow it.

Previous page: **A**ctor Joe Don Baker as Inspector Brimmer.

Panther Party. Although the BPP did later join forces with the white radicals, they felt it was psychologically important for black folks to liberate themselves. The executive said he understood, leaned back in his chair, and repeated that the script lacked a strong role for a white star. He admitted that while minorities are used to being poorly represented in films or not at all, members of the majority or dominant culture are not accustomed to such treatment.

He pointed out that with something like a rap intensive-in-the-hood flick, or a comedy, you could get away without one, but ethnic-themed political films needed big stars to sustain them. Although it's common knowledge the civil rights movement was led by activists like Dr. King and Stokeley Carmichael, *Mississippi Burning* features two compassionate white FBI agents fighting for black rights. Virtually every Vietnam film has had white stars. He asked us if we thought a mainstream audience would have cared about Native American rights without Kevin Costner in the middle of *Dances with Wolves.* "In all honesty," he said, "white people care when white heroes are centrally involved. Politics is a hard sell, ethnic politics is a harder sell, and ethnic politics without a white box office draw is damn near an impossible sell."

He suggested we could create an outspoken Berkeley student, a Mario Savio type that a Tom Cruise could play. "This student could teach the Panthers to stand up for themselves, to believe in themselves. He could turn them on to all that revolutionary literature they read, and because he's white, he's forced to stay in the background to politically guide them."

Silence again . . . I knew my dad was on the verge of revolutionary implosion, but this conversation had become so surreal I had to see how far it could go. "So, the white character is sort of a coach and the Panthers would be like a black militant basketball team battling the forces of oppression?"

"Exactly," he responded. "And their ability to follow his guidance proves they're not racists. The white audience will see themselves positively represented and central to the movement. If we're lucky, they'll come, and black people are gonna come anyway 'cause it's the Black Panthers." Then he pointed out that although Martin Luther King preached freedom and Malcolm X lectured revolution, neither of them ever picked up guns and faced off with white cops! "Regardless of what the historical truth was," he said, "you're talking about the most feared black militant group in American history, period. Most suburban white people thought the Panthers wanted to take what we had. We thought they hated us. There is simply no way to do this film about a group of armed, supposedly antiwhite revolutionaries without the film itself being perceived as antiwhite unless there's a white star on that poster, at least not at this studio."

I remember Pops and I walked in silence for a while as we left that studio. I suppose I felt that perhaps I had let Dad down on some level. Not me personally as a filmmaker, or as his son, but as a friend who had encouraged him to try again. To hope again, to roll this big-ass development boulder up this studio mountain just one more time. I had convinced him that just maybe Hollywood had evolved since the 1970s, that we could do it right this time. We could bring the vision forth intact, politically uncompromised. The old man had flown out from New York on his own dime at a time when neither one of us had much bread. What's more, I'm sure he didn't want to

jeopardize what few studio relationships I had by calling that executive a spineless, time-wasting son of a bitch like he probably wanted to. There wasn't much either of us needed to say. I put my arm around his shoulder. He smiled, and we continued walking through the back lot. I thought about that verse from Kipling's poem "If":

If you can dream—and not make dreams your master;
If you can think—and not make thoughts your aim;
If you can meet with Triumph and Disaster
And treat those two impostors just the same . . .

Pops and I were familiar with both impostors. Being rejected at a studio was far from disaster. In fact, it's the norm. But what that executive said was a political barometer; clearly we were in trouble. We had arrived at the car Dad had borrowed from a friend. A bright red Rabbit with a cheery interior decor that seemed a strange juxtaposition to our mood. The L.A. sun was setting and Dad was due to catch the red-eye back to the Big Apple. He paused, took his funky cigar out, and actually lit it. Pops rarely lights up. "Well," he said, "what you wanna do now, son?" I hesitated, then replied, "I think we do all we can, give up what we have to financially, and do this without compromising the integrity of the piece. And if we fail . . . then we don't do it at all . . . What are your thoughts?" Dad paused, took a drag on his cigar, and said, "I'm with you, son . . . I agree."

That was about five years after the train ride when my Pops had first read me his take on the Panther story. It would be another four years and several rejections later before we would finally find a company willing to give our vision a shot. By this time I had directed *New Jack City* for Warners and *Posse* for Working Title/Polygram. *Posse* had done enough numbers-wise to get me invited back to the cinematic picnic, and for the first time I found myself able to pick my next film. Against the advice of most, I chose *Panther*.

In the end we did have to give up everything we could financially to get the piece done, but we managed to keep our original vision intact. We didn't force the Panther story through a Caucasian character's point of view. We didn't soften the politics or water it down. For better or worse, the film we made was the film we set out to make.

BROTHER FROM ANOTHER PLANET

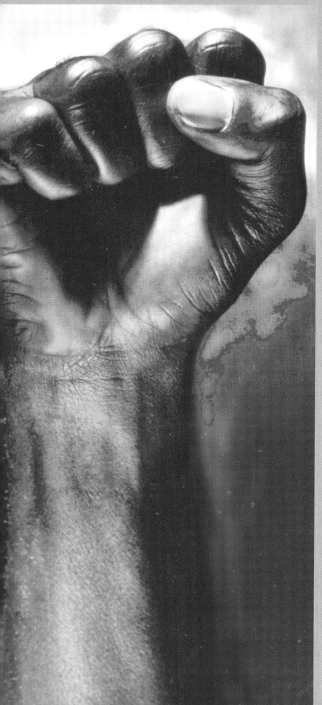

Perhaps at this point I should make one disclaimer and one confession. First, unless otherwise indicated, the following philosophies are simply my opinions and I take the blame for them solely. I share them in hopes of shedding light on the cinematic choices we made while filming *Panther*.

Second, I'm an optimistic pessimist. Although it seems to me that humankind is going the way of the dinosaur, I like to believe our often feeble cinematic attempts at enlightenment can occasionally make a difference. Like the rest of my family, I seem to find a certain humor in the tragic human condition that affects not only my filmmaking but my views on life as well. Ultimately this movie we have shot will not only be perceived as a stand against oppression but also as a stand against racism. So perhaps it's best if I just come clean with my views on race early on.

I think my outlook on race was shaped first and foremost by my two nonconformist, nonmaterialistic, interracial avant-garde crazy-ass parents, who made an in-your-face art of kicking down almost any racist or sexist barriers placed before them. Unlike their bohemian peers who talked stuff about traveling the world with little more than a backpack, my hip parents were globe trotters who picked up and hit the road with two children and almost no money.

From Mexico and Morocco to Amsterdam and Paris on a student's budget, we saw people of all races, cultures, and religions, most living thoroughly convinced that theirs was the one true or righteous lifestyle. Most of them believing that their religion, or race, or social outlook somehow was inherently superior to their neighbors.

When you travel you see that everywhere the colonialists went they spread their toxic self-serving "white is right" mentality. But you also see clearly that rich black Haitians will kill poor black Haitians. East Indian Hindus will kill East Indian Muslims of the exact same color. British fight the Irish and vice versa, even at a soccer match.

There have been studies that show that man, basically a hunter-gatherer, does not live well in groups of more than forty. Beyond forty we tend to subdivide, although we are social animals. Living in cities of millions of people is absolutely unnatural. Once you

I played a small cameo as Stokeley Carmichael. He has a unique oratory style, is a brilliant public speaker, and this "We Are at War" speech is vintage Stokeley. I am often asked why I didn't play Huey Newton myself; the answer is twofold. One, we were covering the early years when Newton was about twenty-one. Two, with all of the jealousies that exist in our country, I didn't want my playing Newton to get misconstrued as a vanity piece. My ego was not in six more close-ups of Mario—the project was bigger than all of us.

recognize man's unfortunate tendency toward global tribalism, it's easier to step outside your own particular cycle of repression and view one's situation with some objectivity. This objectivity or realization that perhaps you as the individual are not "the target" helps empower you to deal with, rather than simply react to, racism or repression on any level.

Ironically, it seems that African American leaders become more of a threat when they develop an international outlook on race. Malcolm X, when he echoed the Black Muslim doctrine of whites being "blue-eyed devils," probably did more to swell the ranks of the KKK than he did to threaten the status quo. When Malcolm X returned from Mecca, however, reporting that he had prayed with Muslims of all colors and that perhaps the color of a person's skin was of less significance than where the heart was at, he became a threat on a whole new level. Unfortunately, his life was cut short soon after. The Black Panthers were probably less of a threat when they

could be criminalized in the media as "Armed Antiwhite Hate Mongers." But the Panthers forged alliances with the Chicanos (Brown Berets, Young Lords, etc.), the Asians (Red Peril), and the White Radical Left (SDS—Students for a Democratic Society—as well as the Peace and Freedom Party). Not only did they form a united color front against the Vietnam War, but they also ran Panther Eldridge Cleaver for president and Jerry Rubin from the Peace and Freedom Party for vice president. Black and white on the same ticket!

This solidifying of the Panthers with the radical left was extremely disconcerting to the powers that be. In fact, J. Edgar Hoover stated that the Panthers posed one of the greatest threats to America's security, and declared them Public Enemy No.1.

REACHING THE PEOPLE

Although *Panther* will probably be classified as a political thriller, I didn't want anyone to feel that they should get three college credits for sitting through the damn thing. As Clint Eastwood said when we shot *Heartbreak Ridge*, "Whip me, beat me, but don't bore me." If *Panther* works as I hope, its as "edutainment," not as a documentary. The movie had to move, to have a flow, a rhythm, and, yeah, some humor. If the film rocks, if it not only informs but entertains as well, then maybe, just maybe, the kids might go, not just the folks who know, not just the baby boomers who remember, but the young brothers and sisters who need it most. Like the one in our early test marketing for the film who said he thought "Huey Newton" was a cookie.

We need to reach the gang members who inherited the bravado of the Panthers without the political ideology to understand that their own behavior is often counterrevolutionary. If the film is entertaining and can reach what Karl Marx called the "lumpenproletariat"—the brothers and sisters on the block—without compromising its integrity, then we have gone beyond preaching to the choir. Me, my Pops, Preston Holmes, and all the other good folks involved in the filmmaking process will undoubtedly slap each other five, 'cause we got a tough movie done, and anyone who knows filmmaking knows that that in itself is a triumph. But it's not about us, it's about an opportunity to send a little power to the people. "Each one, teach one."

I think that film is most powerful when it is inclusive, not exclusive. When it taps into something classic in human nature and in doing so helps us articulate something about ourselves. When the cinematic magic works, we extend far beyond our own plasticity, beyond the race, sex, or age of the protagonist. We identify as part of the human experience.

Ultimately, the Black Panther Party was an indelible part of American history. To do the movement justice, I can only hope that the film, like the Party, has an emotional resonance that exceeds color lines. David Hilliard, who headed the BPP after Huey, once told me that they believed in "Black Power" but not at the expense of any other race. After all, it was the Panthers who coined the phrase "All power to the people." As Chairman Bobby Seale said, "You can't fight racism with racism."

Jerry Rubin appears briefly in the film as an attorney for the Panthers. The Peace and Freedom Party and the Panthers joined forces to run a black and a white candidate on the same ticket—Eldridge Cleaver for president of the United States; Jerry Rubin for vice president. Later, the outspoken Rubin would be tried for conspiracy, along with Bobby Seale, Abbie Hoffman, Tom Hayden, Rennie Davis, Dave Dellinger, Lee Weiner, and John Froines in the notorious Chicago Eight/Seven trial. They were bogusly charged with crossing state lines to incite a riot at the 1968 Democratic National Convention in Chicago. Jerry Rubin was tragically killed in a traffic accident shortly after appearing in our film.

In addition to my father and me calling in all of our cumulative thirty-odd years of cinematic markers to get this picture done, we received invaluable help from all kinds of folks in the political world. California State assemblywoman Barbara Lee, Speaker of the California State Assembly Willie Brown, U. S. congressman Ron Dellums, and many others helped us gain access to locations where film crews are rarely allowed. The two most difficult locations to secure were the Oakland Bay Bridge, below, and the state capitol in Sacramento. God, politics, and weather were permitting, and we were able to film them all.

CULT OF PERSONALITY

I knew when we embarked on this project that undoubtedly a lot of attention would be sucked up in the same old cult of personality sand trap. The Panthers make an easy target for those more interested in character assassination than political evaluation, for those who would focus on the messenger rather than the message. The subliminal message of the older, perhaps more civilized civil rights groups such as the NAACP and the religious Rev. King seemed to say "be better," "be more just," "be more noble" than your enemy, and he will undoubtedly see the error of his ways. "Forgive your oppressor, for they know not what they do." The Panthers never claimed to be saints. They were young, raw, flawed, up-from-the-streets brothers and sisters whose message was clearly that after four hundred years of practice, the oppressor knows exactly what he's doing. Part of their appeal was that they were a real voice, they were imperfect, just human beings, products and victims of the very ghettos they attempted to lead. Who better to motivate a street-level grassroots revolution than revolutionaries who intrinsically understood those streets? Almost all the criticism of the BPP focuses not on their politics but on the personalities of the party leadership.

J. Edgar Hoover is also portrayed in the film. There is substantial evidence to support the theory that the Mob had Hoover fixed, most likely through blackmail having to do with Hoover's homosexuality. Hoover would spy on anyone who displeased him—from Eleanor Roosevelt to JFK. He'd go after an occasional John Dillinger with much fanfare. He'd even go so far as to declare the Black Panther Party "Public Enemy No. 1." But he continually denied the very existence of a Mafia in this country. Mob boss Carmine "The Doctor" Lombardozzi said, "J. Edgar Hoover was in our pocket. He was no one we had to fear." Over one hundred million dollars of taxpayers' money was expended for COINTELPRO, over seven million of it allocated for 1976 alone to pay off informants and provocateurs. That's twice the amount spent in the same period by the FBI to pay off organized crime informants. However, it was not Hoover's sexual preferences that made him a foe. I did not care to focus on his personal life any more than I did on the Panthers'.

What I do care about is that these bad up-from-the-streets brothers and sisters

showed us we could stand up to police brutality. What I care about is that this self-educated, bold, lawbook-reading Huey P. Newton had the gall to use the oppressors' laws to fend off the oppressor at a time when black folks were getting shot for even thinking about getting off their knees. Were the Panthers part gangster? Part hoodlum? Hell, any group who cares to, dares to, and is able to mobilize brothers from the hood better know something. To take the revolution to the street? To discipline the undisciplined? To organize the unorganized? People who have been conditioned to fail, conditioned to come late, conditioned to disrespect themselves, conditioned to mistrust, dance, prance, talk shit, rap, tap, play ball, sing, swing, get high, self-destruct, and do everything but think politically? Yeah, to deal with that part of us, the raw, uncut, up from the street us, you better be bad. If you're not, then get back to home base before you get hurt and dream of a tidy revolution where no one gets their hands dirty, and theorize, and write, and criticize, and debate along with the other "armchair revolutionaries," as the Panthers dubbed them.

Page 142: **A** film scene of a group on the lawn of the Sacramento State Capitol watching the Panthers approach.
Above: The crew ready to film.
Right: Actor Marcus Chong as Huey Newton strikes one of the Punk Panthers played by Aklam.

I remember once as a kid I walked into my dad's office on the twelfth floor. He had some cat who owed him money hanging out the window by his legs. Now, was that a professional way to conduct business? Was it karmically a sound thing to do? Would small claims court (which he had already tried) help a minority businessman collect? Do I condone this sort of behavior? The answer to all the above is unequivocally, no. But let me say this: That guy left town owing a lot of folks money, but Melvin Van Movies got paid. And my college tuition got paid. Maybe I'll be fortunate enough to deal on a higher level than Pops had to coming up, but if I do, it's owed to him.

There were several pseudo-revolutionary groups during the late 1960s and 1970s. Unlike the Panthers, few of them had a real platform or functional political agenda to put into effect. Black was now becoming "beautiful" and "talking revolution" was in vogue. The BPP considered most of these theo-reticians to be "armchair revolutionaries." Our "Punk Panthers" was a composite group based on cultural nationalists, the San Francisco Paper Panthers, and the bald-headed rivals of the Panthers known as the United Slaves (US).

I had worked with Richard Dysart on *L.A. Law.* Richard was already familiar with Hoover and nailed his clipped speech pattern and tightly wound mannerisms. We enhanced Richard's lower cheeks slightly, giving him Hoover's bulldog jowls.

My education was not about Mario; it's about some black folks who threw some bricks so brothers like me could even apply to universities, let alone graduate. Isn't the dynamic clear? If Martin Luther King was the carrot, Malcolm was the stick. Both equally interdependent halves of the same revolutionary coin. If the civil rights movement was the good cop, the Panthers and the Black Power movement were the tough cop. They were the psychological enforcers with the implied, not real, threat of what could be if the establishment continued to repress us.

Because brothers and sisters like the Panthers fought, died, hustled, boycotted, and organized, we can sit around and write our nice books and make our movies about a struggle that will never literally cost us our blood. We'll probably never be political prisoners spending record-breaking amounts of time in solitary confinement, as Brother Huey P. Newton did. We'll never be bound and gagged in a court of law until our gums bleed, as Bobby Seale was. And we'll probably never be murdered in our sleep next to our pregnant lady, as Fred Hampton was by Chicago police. We probably won't be beaten, jailed, shot at, and spied on because of what we stand for, as the Panthers were. And if we're criticized, hopefully we won't be unfairly criticized twenty years later by those who have no idea what it's like to be in a war.

Huey Newton, Jimi Hendrix, Janis Joplin, and many other 1960s icons would die drug-related deaths. Few would retroactively attempt to invalidate Hendrix's musical legacy, but Newton's political one would be a constant target. Perhaps we can accept a black rock star a whole lot easier than a black revolutionary.

Bobby Seale became a teacher. David Hilliard, an author, is still politically active. Elaine Brown is still involved with the movement; she is an author and lives in France. Kathleen Cleaver is a lawyer, and Eldridge Cleaver, still as fiery as ever, resides in Oakland. Take six people, most of whom are from the hood, and if four or five of that six make it, those are damn good odds. Factor into the equation the physical trials and the psychological tribulations that these folks endured, and those are super odds.

POWER TO THE PEOPLE

The broader message that the Panthers gave their lives for, the message that often gets lost in the hype to sell newspapers, is simple. The Panthers called for "Black Power to Black people, White Power to White people, Red Power to Red people, Yellow Power to Yellow people, and Brown Power to Brown people. All power to the people." The message clearly is about self-empowerment. A simple message, albeit a dangerous one to a military-industrial complex invested in keeping the races separate and classes dependent. I felt this Power to the People doctrine was key to the Panther story. Consequently, it's reflected in almost every aspect of the film, from the casting and lighting to the rhythm and score of the picture.

If *Panther* was didactic, preachy, a history lesson, or a glorified documentary, we'd lose. The core audience would sneak next door and watch *Rambo Stays Home Alone, Part VII.* Hollywood would say, "I told you so," and the next brother or sister who tried to tackle an African American historical piece without rap music, singing, or black folks shuffling would have it that much tougher. The piece had to work as a film, as a story about human beings. However, if we based the story solely on any one party leader's point of view, the key empowerment message could be eclipsed or invalidated by that leader's personal idiosyncrasies and the inevitable character assassinations that would follow. I believe the movement ultimately was greater than the sum of its parts.

Even though the film was titled *JFK*, director Oliver Stone never dealt with Kennedy's personal life dramas. He never even debated JFK's politics; he kept the focus exactly where he wanted it, on the conspiracy to assassinate a president and its resulting coup d'etat. The audience and the press would have to deal squarely with the conspiracy issue and evaluate the film on that basis rather than the subjective pros and cons of John F. Kennedy's politics or personality.

If the media make a "media god" out of Malcolm X and then put a bullet in him, to some extent it kills his movement as well. If the media make gods of JFK or Martin and then they're assassinated, the same thing occurs. But when it came to the Panthers, a different dynamic seemed to be at play. Fred Hampton, chairman of the Chicago Panther chapter, said, "They can jail the revolutionary, but they can't jail the revolution. They can kill the man but not the movement."

For some reason, when Brother Huey seemed to be getting the lion's share of the press, Bobby Seale would appear in the news leading the Panthers to the state capitol while Huey remained back in Oakland. When Bobby got in the limelight, suddenly Eldridge appeared on the scene, or Hilliard, or some other Panther was stepping into the media focus. Did the Panthers understand the importance of not letting any one man become a media island? Jailing Huey over the Officer Frey shooting did not jail the revolution. In fact, just the opposite occurred. Before Huey's incarceration there were approximately seventy-five Panthers. At his release, there were about five thousand.

If the Panthers themselves had been ingenious enough to delegate power and in effect insulate any one leader from becoming the definitive Panther media god, we as filmmakers would attempt to do the same.

By using the composite character of Judge to carry us through the film, my father's script enables the viewer to experience the key historical events with the various leaders involved. It also affords us an overall view of the larger FBI drug plot and subplots that we would not otherwise be privy to.

Often, biographies based on charismatic leaders create a subliminal division where we the audience view the hero as "other," as Messiah-like, as greater than we. I felt using a rank-and-file member such as Judge as a protagonist subliminally empowered the Everyman, underscoring the "Power to the People" theme. As an average guy, Judge seems somehow closer to us; his heroic acts seem more achievable. If we could just get a couple members of a modern-day largely apathetic audience to believe that they, too, could make a difference? Hey, I'm happy.

When the Panthers made the color-blind choice of Charles Garry to defend Huey, they lost some of their less open-minded black support. Newton affectionately dubbed Garry the "Lenin of the courtroom." Robert Culp played Charles Garry, who defended Huey against the charges that he murdered Officer Frey. Ironically, Robert's son and my friend, Joe Culp, played Frey in the movie. Doing any historical piece requires extensive research. Doing a piece where the people involved are living and often broken into various factions is akin to walking through a minefield. Most of the court scene was based on actual transcripts from the trial. Almost all of the speeches in the movie are taken verbatim from the recorded material.

HISTORY AND OURSTORY

When we were first trying to fund *Panthers*, some studio executive who probably doesn't realize he should remain nameless told me, "Black people obviously don't like history because not enough of them went to see *Glory*. No matter how good a picture is, most nine-to-five hard working black folks ain't trying to get beat up all week just to go out Friday night and spend seven bills to watch some of the finest black ac-

tors following a young white boy's orders and getting their asses shot off on account of it. If you can manipulate a people into believing that all they were historically were slaves, butlers, and mammies, they are going to tell you with their box-office vote where you can shove that version of history. Who wants to hear that stuff during Miller time? As my Pops says, "History is a book written by the winner." Well, we damn sure ain't winning when we're not telling our own history and our people know it.

I can't tell you how many times nice, well-meaning liberal white folks have hit on me and Dad with some incredible true story that we've "just got to do." Why? Because its about some real-life black person so talented, so brave, with a heart of gold. Unfortunately, the evil forces of racism kept him down and he suffered greatly (albeit nobly) and ended up penniless, alone, and dead. Pleeeaze man, most black folks are tired of that stuff. We know all about the price of standing up. We know that whether you're Martin Luther King and say "Freedom by peaceful means" or Malcolm X and say, "Freedom by any means necessary," they will kill you both. They'll name a holiday after one man, but they'll kill you both. Most of us realize that unfortunately the covert agencies seem to have made good on that promise. Elaine Brown pointed out in *A Taste of Power* that after the deaths of Malcolm and Martin, the FBI was going to do their best to ensure "there would be no more black Messiahs" unless they created one.

Eldridge Cleaver described to me in detail a confrontation that took place between the Panthers and the police in front of *Ramparts* magazine. Eldridge, the author of *Soul on Ice*, had been commissioned to interview Betty Shabazz (the recently widowed wife of Malcolm X) for the magazine. Since Malcolm's death and the possible government-Muslim involvement, security for Ms. Shabazz was a major concern. The Black Panthers were there to protect her personally. Cleaver, who witnessed the scene, describes it even more intensively than it appears in the film: "Brother Newton knew the law, spoke the law, and when that pig trying to intimidate him flinched as if to go for his gun Newton, dared him to draw." Eldridge said, "Man, when Huey, finally disgusted with that pig, spun on his heels and strutted away, he looked like diamonds were popping from his shoes."

The Panthers didn't just talk. They started patrolling the police long before video cameras and Rodney King. They took pictures of police "interacting" on minorities during a time when few of the good people outside of the hood could fathom the police being anything less than "just." They read victims their rights and sometimes they even posted their bail. They started the food and breakfast programs, the free-shoe giveaways, the busing to prisons, the free medical clinics, sickle cell anemia testing, and later even some award-winning schools.

"I'd rather die on my feet than live on my knees" is one of my favorite lines in the film. It's told by Huey Newton to Judge. Ultimately, Panthers did die for the movement, and ultimately we were not out to make another black folks-dying-as-usual *Glory*-type flick. However, while they were on their feet, while they stood, they stood so strong, so tough, that the effect was nothing less than electrifying to a largely downtrodden black community.

For all that and more, we forgive them their trespasses. We forgive them for being raw, and proud, and young, and flawed, and human, and, yes, we even forgive them for their mortality.

The Panthers, greatly inspired by Malcolm X, put into effect Malcolm's "do for self" doctrine. Often we African American filmmakers are encouraged to compete. I thought it would be interesting to salute not only Malcolm as the Panthers did, but also to salute brother Spike Lee's casting choice of the regal Angela Basset as Betty Shabazz, Malcolm's wife. In this scene, Betty Shabazz is escorted by the Panthers after being interviewed by Eldridge Cleaver at *Ramparts* magazine.

TIMELINE

We had chosen the protagonist through which we see the historical events and characters. But what events and time span should be covered? In spite of Nixon's Attorney General John Mitchell's statements in *Newsweek* magazine that the Justice Department would wipe out the Black Panther Party by the end of 1969, the Party continued until 1982. With forty-four chapters in different states, all with various leaders, we realized we would have to pick a specific period of time to cover or risk doing great injustice to their rich history.

The old man and I knew we wanted to capture the genesis of the party in Oakland. Thus the question was really where to end the film. Pops decided to end our story around 1969-70. This is before Hoover and the FBI's secret COINTELPRO war to discredit, divide, and neutralize the BPP really took heavy casualties. It's before Newton was released from prison, wrote any of his books, and got his doctorate. It's also before the Party became almost Felliniesque, with Newton (like too many folks in the 1960s) falling ironically to drugs, and before Eldridge's public split from the Party. It's prior to Bobby Seale getting kidnapped and literally dragged across country to be tried as a conspirator in the notorious "Chicago Eight Trial."

Besides choosing the early years to cover, because they were admittedly more inspiring, this was the same period where our own family history intersected with the Panthers. We felt it was the time span the Van Peebles boys were most qualified to cover.

FINALLY OAKLAND

We sped along the freeway in one of those chunky big-ass rent-a-vans. The sign whizzing by read, OAKLAND NEXT EXIT.

This was it, man, Oakland, birthplace to the "Black Panther Party for Self-Defense." Oakland, where thousands of African Americans had migrated from the South to work the industrial jobs, only to be displaced and forgotten years later as America moved into the technological age. Oakland, whose huge shipping port was one of the largest in the nation; Oakland, where drugs, as in most American ghettos, had left their scars; and Oakland, the city across the bay from San Francisco, where I grew up and now was actually location-scouting for a feature on the legendary Black Panthers.

I've never taken filmmaking for granted. Perhaps I had an all-too-sobering view of the so-called 1970s Black Exploitation era vis-à-vis my dad's turbulent career. It's abundantly clear to me that if Hollywood makes several Vietnam films that eventually don't perform financially, no one says white films aren't making money. They attribute this economic failure to the theme or genre of the pictures but not the race of the actors or filmmakers involved. In the 1970s, however, we found ourselves locked in a cinematic catch-22 that eventually produced and saturated the market with flicks like *Superfly Comes Back from Disneyland, Part III* and *Shaft Goes to the Seven-Eleven, Part IV.* When these genre pictures eventually ran their course, Hollywood proclaimed that black films were no longer making money. Black exploitation exemplified.

As quickly as they had opened, the financial doors shut to black filmmakers, actors, and technicians with a resounding clang. These doors would be reluctantly leveraged open almost twenty years later, ironically by the very kids who as youngsters saw those exploitation flicks and never realized the Hollywood dream was not intended to include them.

Most directors know that the opportunities to direct don't present themselves indefinitely. But this is especially the case if you're not a member of the dominant culture that controls studios, distribution, theater chains, and everything

Painstaking attention was paid to detail. Photos and stock footage were literally going to be interwoven into the body of the film. So our actors had to match, not only in terms of props and wardrobe, but in physical placement relative to each other and in attitude. Bobby Hutton seemed to wear a variety of hats, often cocked at cool, defiant angles. Here our actor matched not only his style, but the specific way in which Lil' Bobby Hutton carried his rifle. The Panthers, who knew that the authorities would use any and every excuse to bust them, were well versed in gun laws. (Weapons had to be pointed up or down at all times and carried in plain view). The wardrobe department matched details down to Bobby Seale's one black glove, with the proclamation

he had come to read in his left hand. Ronald Reagan, then governor of California, was on the capitol lawn talking with a student group when the the real Panthers marched up. We used actual film footage of Reagan on the lawn in the movie. The actor who played the door guard, overwhelmed by the Panthers arrival, was visiting his father the day the real Panthers marched into the capitol. His father was the actual guard on duty in 1967. Although our guard in the movie was just a kid at the time, he was able to describe in detail what went down that day. He said that the Panthers' unexpected visit caused a major panic that sent the state trooper budget for the year sky-rocketing.

down to the popcorn and Gummi Bears we eat. Cinematically, the dominant culture is still predominantly the landlord; we are like tenants as long as we're paying the rent, cool. But as the 1970s showed, we can always be asked to leave. Now, this is nothing to get bitter about. It just means you change what you can change, while you've got the power to change it. Make each film count, aware that it could be, and one day will be, your last. As my Pops says, "When you finally get into the kitchen you might as well cook something you like, because sometimes you're the only one eating it." Pops and I have lost our money on films together, and made money together, and in both cases it feels a hell of a lot better if the project in question has some emotional resonance for us.

Though conventional Hollywood wisdom was against a black political period piece performing economically, doing *Panther* made absolute sense to the Van Peebles boys. That first day in Oakland, riding in the van with the various department heads on our maiden location scout, was a victory.

Almost as if this raggedy van had somehow taken nine long years to finally reach Oakland. Yeah, the revolution would not only be televised as the "Last Poets" didn't say, it would be filmed in living color! My man Preston, coproducer, had on his shades, looking like a cool refugee from *Shaft*. Pop was low riding in the front seat Chicago-style, with his old chewed-up stogie as usual. Eddie Pei, our director of photography, was perched on the edge of his seat like an alert Asian schoolboy taking everything in. Richard Hoover, our production designer, was waving his hands in the backseat as he bitched about not having more of a budget. But today, man, nothing could faze me; we had arrived. I'd have even thrown on my black leather "Wanna be a Panther" jacket as homage to brother Huey if it weren't so damn hot.

We cruised down Market Street snapping photos of the old Panther headquarters, which is now a bakery. A blue Toyota drove slowly past us. Aside from being too noisy with traffic to record clean dialogue for the movie, Market Street had changed significantly since 1966-67, which is when our picture begins. The most significant change is BART (Bay Area Rapid Transit). The sleek commuter train supported by a massive cement highway in the sky runs right over the old Market Street, literally zooming over the ghetto, casting everything below in its shadow. Obviously we would have to recreate the Panther Party headquarters somewhere else. Additional builds would tax Richard's already tight construction budget. Naturally, this sent Richard's small hands aflying again, mussing up his already staticky blond hair. Having worked with everyone in the van before and knowing Richard's talents as a production designer, I had come to regard this hair-raising ritual as a good omen.

"That's Merritt College up ahead on the right," exclaimed our city-appointed guide. As we grabbed up our cameras and pulled to a stop, I noticed that same blue Toyota cruise by yet again. Merritt College had been abandoned for several years, a casualty of urban economics. Apparently the city felt higher learning for inner-city youth was no longer in the budget. So the college where thousands of black students, among them Bobby Seale and Huey P. Newton, had gotten an affordable education was boarded up and now in danger of being bulldozed into a parking lot or some such thing. As Richard snapped a couple more location shots that same mystery Toyota made a U-turn, pulled up several yards behind us, and stopped. I glanced over to Pop to see if he was catching any of this. He was. For several minutes no one exited the Toyota. Our guide, oblivious, continued to explain the history of the college to Eddie Pei while Richard snapped away.

Slowly, two figures exited the Toyota— both African-American women in their mid-forties. Both wore dark shades, and both were armed with serious attitude. They eyed Richard suspiciously as they marched up to us.

The more aggressive of the two sisters took her stance like one

The Panthers were a youth movement. Lil' Bobby Hutton was seventeen. Tarika, the first woman to join, was about sixteen. Fred Hampton, head of the Illinois chapter, was eighteen. Huey Newton was in his early twenties; Bobby Seale was in his late twenties, and Eldridge Cleaver was in his early thirties. Sometimes leaders such as King, Gandhi, and even Malcolm X can come off as larger than life, far greater than us. The Panthers' appeal, however, was not as saints but as young, flawed, homegrown revolutionaries. We felt this youth element was important to today's often apathetic young audience, who rarely see themselves as politically empowered. "It only takes one grain of sand to move the world."

HUEY P. NEWTON

"Know what I hate more than anything? Givin' blood. And I mean I hate it. If one of my kids got into an accident and needed some blood, I'd have to think about it, you dig? And some nurse wavin' some big needle near my arm? Naw, I mean I hate givin' blood, YOU DIG," exclaimed Dick Gregory, looking like a Black Moses in a suit. I had stopped in to check on Mr. Gregory on my way to the jail set. We needed to start filming seventeen minutes ago, but a generator had blown and two actors were late. Tarika was already getting the actors and extras warmed up marching and chanting. Word had gotten out quickly that lazy-ass L.A. extras didn't last long on our set. We had everyone drilling constantly, because everyone from principal to background counted. They had to become Panthers. Budget constraints being what they were, all we could afford for on-set accommodations for Gregory was the usual honey wagon (honey wagons aptly named not because they were sweet accommodations, but because their cramped, little separate compartments call to mind the image of bees tucked tightly into their honeycombs). Gregory's room was at least seventeen inches wider than one of those handicapped toilet stalls. Now in his sixties, the legendary comedian, dietitian, and political activist Dick Gregory was a seminal member of the civil rights movement. I had come to welcome him and offer him my dad's and my director's room, an all-purpose trailer just marginally larger than his room. "You kidding me, you think I'm soft?!" he sputtered. "Sheeet, this room is like the Taj Mahal compared to

some of the places we had to stay in during the movement. Like I said, I hate givin' blood, but if Melvin Van Peebles needed some, I wouldn't hesitate, understand?! I knew the son-of-a-bitch didn't have any capital when he called me, I know your daddy, boy! Hell, I'm surprised you two raised the capital to do the Panther story at all! Seriously!" He then leaned in conspiratorially and pointed to his script. "This stuff here is the history they don't want America to know about. Go on, tell our history. Don't worry about me. I've waited sixty years to see us get these opportunities, I can wait another hour!"

Gregory was a trip. The older sisters and brothers had heart, man. They knew the deal. There you have Dick Gregory, who stood up to the Mob and the establishment, arriving twenty minutes early— ready, willing, and able. And I got young cats, actors, lucky to be acting, showing up late??!! Cats my age and younger, who don't know what it's about. No bad intentions, most of them just don't comprehend the struggle before them— the struggle it took to get us shots like this. Part of what this movie is about is showing that struggle. Just sixty years ago, if we were lucky enough to act at all, we'd be relegated to shuffling butlers and mammyhood, as opposed to revolutionaries.

Gregory had referred publicly to Hoover as "one of the most dangerous men in this country and said that the Mob were lower than snakes." Hoover sent orders to "neutralize" Gregory and suggested that perhaps they could get La Casa Nostra to take care of him. Gregory, unlike many others, survived.

used to confrontation: "Where are you from?" The subtext was clear. "And why don't y'all get the hell back there?" Meanwhile, Bold Soul Sister No.2 seemed to be focusing in on my Pops. "Hey, isn't that Melvin Van Peebles?" Ms. Aggressive Stance peered over her shades, giving Pops the hard-eye once-over. "Sure is," she echoed, her face warming. "Damn, Huey loved your movie *Sweetback*," she grinned. "Pleased to meet you, sisters," Pops said, crooning in that extra-smooth "they recognized me first" baritone. Pops has a special voice reserved for these occasions. Ms. Aggressive spun back on me, her pretty bronzed-colored face suddenly years younger. "And you must be his son Marvin? No, Mario, right?" "Right," I said. "Yeah," she exclaimed like someone who guessed a right answer on a game show. "My name is Tarika, but during the revolution they called me Sister Matilaba, and this," she said, introducing her companion, "is Sister Love."

It turned out that Tarika and Sister Love were on a mission to save Merritt College and one day reopen it. They had mistaken us for city planners or rather destroyers out to reclaim the land. It also turned out that both women were ex-Panthers. Tarika at age sixteen was the first woman to join the party, get armed, and become proficient enough as a weapons expert to train her Panther brothers. The character of Alma, played by Nefertiti in the film, was loosely based on Tarika. I'm always a little suspicious of these war stories as they tend to get embellished, but this whole scenario was later corroborated by none other than Eldridge Cleaver. Eldridge told me he personally bought Tarika her first gun.

Tarika and Sister Love, like most ex-Panthers, are very protective of their unique Panther history. They guard their revolutionary legacy like lionesses guarding their young. And rightfully so, for the Panthers are often victims of media trickology. Witness their unfortunate buffoonlike portrayal in the universally loved *Forrest Gump*.

Our collective cinematic track records and Dad's history with the Panthers proved to be invaluable in terms of gaining their trust. Eventually the Panthers understood that we were not some large Hollywood studio out to exploit their history but rather an African-American-owned film company, MVP Films, working in association with Working Title Films, an independent film company. The other key factor for them and us was that we had been awarded Hollywood's much-coveted "final cut."

We all know that modern-day heavyweight champions are African Americans— Ali, Tyson, Forman. Yet when Hollywood makes its *Rocky* flicks, the champ inevitably ends up looking more like Stallone. It's common knowledge that karate is a martial art developed by Asians, but did anyone think Hollywood was gonna let the karate kid be Japanese? Of the first forty-four settlers of Los Angeles, twenty-six were African Americans, but you rarely see that reflected in any mainstream Westerns.

Without making any judgment as to the merits of these films, one thing is historically clear. No matter what the story, the dominant culture will find a way to impose itself into the foreground. Our being awarded final cut was insurance that we would not have to follow usual Hollywood formulas. It also meant, for better or for worse, the buck stopped with us. We couldn't blame any nebulous studio exec in a suit. Our restraints would be economic in nature, not political. I

Franz Fanon points out that education is often used by the oppressor to teach the oppressed to accept its values. The BPP held political education classes (PE classes) to educated its members about their real history—beyond slavery. After conferring with ex-Panthers, I decided that part of preparing our actors to become Panthers would include PE classes. We would meet in my cramped office to discuss everything from the Ten Points to current Panther biographies and to the philosophies and books that shaped Panther philosophy. The goal was to have the actors so well versed in Panther ideology that they could react as Panthers under any given situation.

California gun laws did not permit citizens on parole to carry a handgun. This is why Newton, who was often on parole, carried his signature shotgun and Bobby Seale got the pistol. The Panther beret was inspired by old French underground movies in which the French Resistance, who wore berets, stood up against the occupying Nazi army. To some extent, the Oakland police conducted themselves like an occupying army.

told Preston that as a matter of policy we should give any hostile armed ex-Panthers dissatisfied with the film my Dad's address.

For years, studios had talked of making a Black Panther movie. Even HBO was making noise, but to date, incredibly, no one had done it. We would be the first and hopefully not the last. We were welcomed in ways that I doubt any other filmmakers would've been. And for that I have to thank the Panthers and credit my Dad.

We ended up spending the entire day with Tarika and Sister Love. These two tireless women led us through "their" Oakland like warriors returning to the battlefield. They pointed out every minute detail down to the bullet holes still left in the wall across from where Lil' Bobby Hutton, the first Panther to die by Oakland police gunfire, was killed. We even met his mother, the gracious Mrs. Hutton, who later appeared in the film, and since has passed away. We saw the famous intersection of 55th and Market where Panthers first rallied to get a stoplight installed. We saw one of the early locations for the food and breakfast programs where sisters like these two helped feed hungry kids. Across the street was the Safeway that Panthers boycotted until it agreed to hire minorities.

We explored the old community church that had been painted by

Pictured here is the character Alma surrounded by the sisters as they join the Party. Before the "women's movement," there were African American female Panther leaders such as Elaine Brown, Erika Huggens, Kathleen Cleaver, and many more. Although the sisters undoubtedly had a tougher road, they were an invaluable part of the movement. They were the backbone of the survival programs and schools. Ex-Panther Sister Love said, "Often I had to tend to Party business while carrying my baby on my hip. Being a mother and a revolutionary were, by no means, mutually exclusive." Ed Eckstein, Adam Kidron and Sam Sap came up with a dynamic song for the Mercury movie sound track produced by Dallas Austin that salutes the female Panther leadership. The record is performed by some of the top female vocalists, who checked their egos at the door and joined musical forces to create the song, "Freedom."

This photo of Huey P. Newton as the serene black warrior was orchestrated by Eldridge and was not a picture that Huey liked. Eldridge Cleaver, minister of information, was an author and journalist; as such he was familiar with the media's power and influence. He also knew that a picture could be worth a thousand words, especially to a semiliterate black readership. Long after the Mulford Act was passed, making it illegal for the BPP to bear arms, the Panther newspaper continued to be published—the pen being mightier than the sword. In the movie, we took artistic license and had Eldridge shoot the picture of Huey in the printing plant—underscoring the need for minorities to control their own imagery, rather than allow their history to be told by the dominant culture.

My father played the wise, old jailbird who speculates and prophesies that if black folks had guns, they'd probably shoot each other. Robi Reed Humes did our casting with the concept of using relatively new young actors as the core Panthers and surrounding them with a veteran support group of more known faces.

Near right: **M**ario as a kid in his father's movie, *Sweet Sweetback's Baadasssss Song.*
Far right: Sweetback on a front page of Panther paper.

the Panthers sometime in 1968. Apparently the old reverend of the church at the time had a fit when these Panthers, many of them mere teenagers, painted his church a vibrant revolutionary red, black, and green with big murals of Malcolm X and Marcus Garvey adorning its front. The church has long since been repainted a socially "safe" dull beige. But the scene inspired by this incident lives on in our film.

"If you look closely, you can still see Garvey and Brother Malcolm shining through the last coat of paint," Sister Love said proudly. "Must be that special Mother Africa paint we used."
"That's right, Sister, the spirits are at work today," added Tarika, half joking as she looked at us. "The spirits are definitely at work."

I had no idea at the time that Tarika and Sister Love along with several other rank-and-file ex-Panthers would end up in the film. In addition to helping us assemble this book, Tarika would become one of our key technical advisers. Ms. Aggressive Stance was a relentless drill instructor who put the actors through their paces endlessly, testing them on the ten points, weapons usage, and marching.

SWEETBACK TO NEW JACK

Back in those days, Tarika, also an accomplished violinist and artist, worked on the Black Panther Party newspaper with Emory Douglas. In fact, Emory, whose classic bold revolutionary artwork seemed to capture the raw power of the movement, laid out the *Sweetback* issue of the paper. (Both Emory's and Tarika's artwork appear during the montage sequences in the film.) In this issue Bobby Seale wrote an introduction to Huey Newton's revolutionary analysis of my father's film *Sweet Sweetback's Baadasssss Song*, which is basically the story of a hustler who evolves into a revolutionary. He's a street brother who moves from the "Me" doctrine to the "We" doctrine. It's important to note that the black exploitation studio-made films that later attempted to ape this formula did not share its revolutionary consciousness. Obviously, to many Panthers who were brothers and sisters from the proverbial "block" striving to elevate their consciousness, *Sweetback* hit a special chord. Discovering this old issue of the paper dedicated to my dad's film blew me away. After all these years of thinking the old man had been exaggerating, if not outright lying, here were the two founders of the Party praising his film's political merit in print. Almost a year earlier I had run into Elaine Brown in Paris. Elaine, who in 1974 had taken up the reins of Party leadership after David Hilliard, had recently published her book, *A Taste of Power*. As striking in person as in her photographs, Elaine had told me that Huey virtually insisted that Panthers go see my Dad's film. But having the actual *Sweetback Panther* issue in my hands brought it all home somehow. Not only had Huey written about old Melvin Van Movies, but inside the newspaper is a faded picture of a small boy who acts in the film. Huey writes about this kid, and the kid happens to be me.

   Interesting that almost twenty years to the month after *Sweetback* became the top-grossing independent hit of 1971, my directorial debut, *New Jack City,* became the most profitable movie for Warner Brothers in 1991. I was one of the young directors to profit directly from the earlier black wave of cinema that my father helped start. So here was Van Peebles' kid after twenty years pulling him back into the cinematic mix with *Panther.* And here were the Panthers, who wrote about us, now having part of their story told by us in one of the most powerful media of the twentieth century, film. As Sister Tarika would say, "The ancestors are busy."

"SWEET SWEETBACK" BLOWS MY MIND EVERYTIME I TALK ABOUT IT BECAUSE IT IS SO SIMPLE AND YET SO PROFOUND.
—HUEY NEWTON

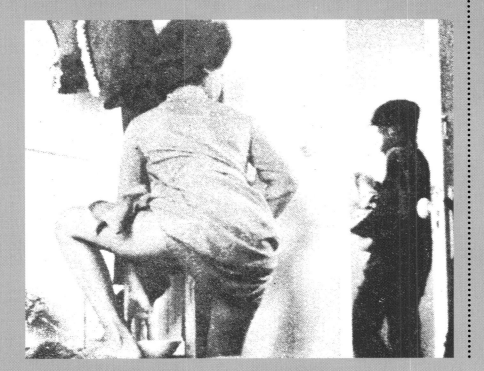

COPS, ROBBERS, & CONSPIRACY

"We gotta get this shot, man! I'm serious, we'll blow our twelve-hour turnaround, and even if we force the actors' call, we need daylight tomorrow, and"—I interrupted Preston, finishing his sentence, —and the cops are gonna shut us down if we try to pull off any more gunfire in a residential area after ten o'clock at night, right?"

"Damn right," Preston answered, popping his eyes and raising his brow in that "I'm serious as a heart attack" way. Preston is on point. It's already five past ten now, and the special-effects person insists she needs five more minutes to rig the extensive gunfire squib hits. If we don't get this damn shot tonight, it's not in the movie, and gunfire is essential to the scene.

We were filming the famous shoot-out where Eldridge Cleaver and Lil' Bobby Hutton got trapped in a basement while the Oakland police fired some two hundred shots into the house and then tear-gassed the place. Eldridge ordered Bobby Hutton to strip before surrendering, reasoning that "pigs probably won't shoot you if you're naked and unarmed. Where are they gonna say you hid the gun?" Teenage Bobby Hutton, perhaps too modest to comply, opted to surrender still clothed, a decision that cost him his life. Bobby was gunned down while surrendering.

With all this in mind, I approached the heavy, ruddy-complexioned silver-haired cop who sat astride his Harley-like hoss. On movie sets we often have to use retired police officers to hold or control traffic, although on both *New Jack* and *Panther*, our main security was FOI (Fruit of Islam). In extreme cases, when you're shooting long late hours and perhaps stretching the limits, the LAPD will pay you a surprise visit, as was our case. This guy was probably a cop when little Bobby Hutton was killed. Hell, he could have been there, for all I know.

"Yer time's up," the officer said pointedly, a trace of edge in his voice.

"Yeah, I know, it's a real waste," I said, trying to come off casual and not focus on the Magnum strapped to his thick waist. "We'll have to derig all the police squib hits."

"What's that mean?" he asked, eyeing our row of 1960s vintage police cars.

"Well, I had wanted the officers to get some good hits in, but we're five minutes

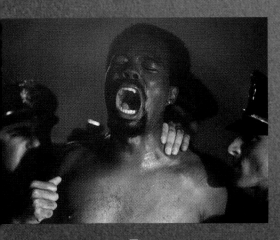

Above: **A**nthony Griffith plays Eldridge Cleaver being restrained by cops as Lil' Bobby is executed.

To Right: Wesley Jonathan playing Lil' Bobby Hutton is mistaken for Seale and shortly after murdered by the Police.

too late," I explained. Preston glanced over at me with that "forget it, brother, we're dead" expression, but he kept his distance, just in case.

"So you're the director or something?" The officer squinted up critically at my lopsided Don King-like Afro. When you're up for twenty-eight hours with no sleep, Afro care becomes a low priority.

"Yeah, but that depends on what critic you talk to." Pause . . . no laugh, not even a chuckle, nothing. Hoss was giving up, no juice.

"So that whole wall is rigged to get shot up by the cops?" he grunted, indicating the small house we had rigged.

"Yes sir, the whole thing," I replied, trying to make it sound exciting as hell.

The officer eyed our Hollywood extra cops as they milled about posturing in period uniform. Then he turned back to me. "Can you blow it in five minutes?"

"I can do it in four." He paused for an eternity, then asked, "If all the cops are here, where and who are the bad guys?" I paused. Good question. Moment of truth? Well, what's needed here is five more minutes, and that's the real truth. "Officer," I replied, "if I tell you that, it would ruin the whole movie for you."

"Yer right," he chuckled. "Take your three minutes." I signaled immediately to Eddie to get all three cameras gunning on this one, two in slow motion, one normal speed…Preston hustled over amped. "What did you tell the guy?"

"I told the pig if he continued to act in a counterrevolutionary fashion I'd have to treat him like a king."

We ducked for cover and started the countdown. The wall blew, the cops applauded, and we managed to make another one of our overly ambitious shooting days without the bond (insurance) company coming down on our asses.

I think the most compelling issue in *Panther* is not whether the Panthers as individuals were good guys or bad guys. As with any group, you probably discover that the truth lies somewhere in between.

BOXER REBELLION?

When old man Melvin Van Movies and I started kicking around the Panther story, he constantly compared the parallel drug subplot with the Boxer Rebellion. Britain fought China over the trade wars and flooded China with opium that addicted the Chinese. Mao Zedong later came along and drove the drugs out. Drugs as a socioeconomic weapon is historically nothing new.

The most controversial and perhaps toughest premise to wrap one's mind around in *Panther* is the concept that police agencies looked the other way while the underworld brought drugs into the minority communities and thus neutralized the alarming rise in

black militancy. For many Americans, this conspiracy of conspiracies, its resulting implications and ripple effects on
today's culture, will be incomprehensible.

In the nineteenth century, President Andrew Jackson
worked hard to remove Native Americans from the southeast-
ern United States. Tens of thousands of Choctaws, Creeks,
and Cherokees, among others, were forcibly marched from
the Carolinas to Oklahoma. They were given blankets infect-
ed with smallpox. Most Americans accept the fact that there
was foul play going on back then but assume nothing like that
could be happening now.

Anyone who knows about the powerful drug and pesticide
industries is probably aware that if the under-budgeted Food
and Drug Administration (FDA) ever gets around actually to
testing and outlawing a chemical or drug, corporations don't
just throw all that expensive product out. They dump it in the

Many circular themes were used throughout the movie. The movie starts with a photo of our two actors outside of the Oakland Panther headquarters, and it ends with the same image, only now it's of the real Huey and Bobby. If film is about creating an alternate reality, a director's job is about creating the best environment for the actors, technicians, and crew to achieve that reality. Ultimately, our job as filmmakers is not camera-intensive or light-intensive; it's people-intensive. I believe that a director's people skills can make a significant difference, especially when you only have thirty-nine days to shoot a historical epic such as *Panther*. Some of the best scenes that I've directed have come when I had the good sense to get out of the way and just catch the magic the actors put out. And sometimes the best ideas come from the cast and crew—it's about being able to listen to your team and yet keep a larger focus. The BPP said, "Power to the People." Part of what I tried to do on the set was to empower the crew, to let them know it was our film and that everyone contributed.

From left to right above:

Michael Wincott as a gangster, James Russo as an FBI agent, and E. Emmet Walsh as an Oakland police authority plot moving drugs into the Oakland black community.

Third World. One of the mad FBI schemes to destroy the Panthers' food and breakfast programs was so preposterous I couldn't use it in the film. A case of truth being far stranger and less believable than fiction.

When speaking of the survival programs, ex-Panther leader Elaine Brown said it best: "We felt that if we gave them food, they might want clothing: if we gave them clothing, they might want housing: if we gave them housing they might want land: and if they got land, they might one day want some abstract thing called freedom."

Hoover and the FBI knew that the most dangerous weapon the Panthers had was not a few guns. Obviously, they would never be equipped to take on the National Guard or army. The BPP's ideological weapon was what the establishment feared most, the psychological effect of people feeding their own, empowering themselves. The BPP's relationship with their community, their grassroots power base is what Hoover dreaded. When police routinely raided BBP headquarters, they would make sure to destroy all the food and breakfast equipment; even the medical supplies would be demolished. The cops would literally be kicking the hell out of a Wonder bread loaf. (We had actual photos of the destroyed offices that we used as research.) Quick flashes of these acts appear in the destruction montage intercut with documentary footage of Kathleen Cleaver as she talked about the nationwide destruction of BBP headquarters by authorities.

The Panthers would receive large donations of food and other perishables, often from mostly white businesses, many of which made their money in the black community. The "poison fruit" plan was proposed by a Newark FBI agent to Hoover. He suggested the bureau laboratory could inject fruit with a laxative-type drug and then write bogus letters convincing the Panthers that the white donors were trying to commit genocide on black children. This was designed to provoke a war between Panthers and the donors. Edgar's office thought the plan "had merit" but ultimately rejected it "because of the lack of control over the treated fruit in transit."

Since long before Prohibition in the United States, there has been a double standard where "laws" and the minority community were concerned. Places like Harlem or Chicago's South Side were dubbed freer zones, where white mobsters were allowed more range to control prostitution, the numbers racket, and gambling. As long as it stayed with the "coloreds," everything was copacetic. This theme even comes up in *The Godfather*. The white gangsters operated directly or through their small-time black counterparts. When an occasional black upstart mobster got too large and tried to take back his own turf, he often found himself suddenly facing the "law."

In the early 1960s, there was some dope in the black community (heroin, coke, reefers etc.). But it remained mostly in the jazz circles and not in great amounts. Outside of the hip music community, drug use was largely frowned upon and stigmatized as "dirty."

As the early 1960s dawned, America seemed to be heading for an identity crisis. After the Korean War, and Senator Joe McCarthy's hysterical Communist-searching, suddenly Americans seemed to be speaking out everywhere. Young white students at Berkeley and African Americans such as Stokeley Carmichael and James Forman of SNCC were all voicing their dissatisfaction. The civil rights movement led by activists such as King (whom Hoover had wiretapped) was marching through the South. Then the anti-Vietnam War movement, and of course, the Black Panther Party for Self-Defense added fuel to the fire.

For the first time, American youth seemed to be rebelling against the very establishment they were due to inherit. They were burning their draft cards, growing their hair, "turning on, tuning in, and dropping out." Worse yet, these young white radical leftists were linking arms with black militants!

Eastern cities had exploded in 1964, Watts in 1965, Cleveland in 1966 and 1967, and then in 1968 King's murder ignited ghettos across America. The National Guard had to be called in. The sky was falling.

The shoot-out with Huey and the Officer Frey was one of the trickiest scenes to recreate. We used models, tech advisers, testimony of ex-Panthers, court transcripts, and Huey's book in order to recreate it. Newton, familiar with the law, describes it in detail, and he poses an interesting question: "Why, if he was under arrest, wouldn't Officer Frey have handcuffed him?" That's standard procedure. Frey, a known racist, had given a talk at a school where he referred to blacks as niggers. Frey was even known to fellow officers as a loose cannon who owned three guns and spent his own money to purchase special high-velocity bullets that destroyed human flesh more than the normal police-issue bullets did.

Kinky, frizzy, full, fine, anything but fake. One of my first directions to the core cast was to let the hair grow, man! I wanted real Afros. It didn't matter if it wasn't any longer than dust on a cue ball. Let it be live. Recreating the 1960s look in a realistic non-campy fashion was a tricky endeavor. Back in the day, companies eager to cash in on the "Black is Beautiful, Peace and Love Era" sold everything from Love Beads and Flower Power bandages to an Afro wig called "Freedom." Our hair, make-up, and wardrobe department did their best to avoid cliches by keeping things as natural as possible. Often make-up and hair departments will use period fashion magazines as references, but these can be deceptive, as they represent trends some people aspired to rather than how everyday folks really looked. We found actual photos of demonstrators, the community, and rank-and-file Panthers to be a much more realistic portrayal. Showing people in an accessible, natural light was especially important because we were portraying the community as the hero.

Above: **A**nthony Griffith and Tracy Costello as Eldridge and Kathleen Cleaver.
Far right: Kadeem Hardison as Judge and Jenifer Lewis as his mother.

What an alarming country the "new America" must have been for paranoid old rightist J. Edgar Hoover, who rose to power with Communist-threat paranoia. His promise to crush the supposedly Communist Panthers had failed. He had jailed many revolutionaries but not the revolution, largely because the Panther power base was the black community itself. The Panthers had mobilized grassroots support. BBP membership was swelling too fast for even the party leadership to grasp. As we say in the film, "There is a Black Panther born every twenty minutes in the ghetto."

Mobsters, as I mentioned earlier, were "connected" with Hoover. The underworld had been bringing illegal alcohol and, then post-Prohibition, narcotics into the minority community for years. They had the experience, the financial motive, and the infrastructure to distribute dope already in place. Hoover might not be able to jail the revolution, but could he medicate it? If the local authorities just looked the other way, if the mob was just given a "little" more freedom in the ghetto, would the Boxer Rebellion effect kick in? Could they pacify this alarming rise in ghetto militancy? Could these Panthers be stopped once and for all if their power base was neutralized? Earl Anthony, a Black Panther FBI informant, in his book, *Spitting in the Wind,* discusses in detail how he was given directly, by the FBI, drugs to distribute.

Elaine Brown writes about visiting Newton during his exile in Cuba. She reports to Newton about Party business, specifically the new Panther school. Pleased, Newton asks if there's any bad news.

"I suppose the dirtiest stuff has to do with a new brand of junior flip but well-armed drug dealers."

"Somebody's got some drugs?"

"It's serious, Huey. Cocaine in Oakland is cheap now, no longer the drug of choice reserved for the rich and famous. It's coming into Oakland at low prices from I don't know where. But can you imagine a white boy in a Rolls riding through the projects? Well, it's happening. Big-time dealers are establishing turf in Oakland through the use of upstart local distributors….You know the cops are in the shit from the outside. Young niggers—sixteen and seventeen years old—were perched on the rooftops with automatic rifles, with scopes yet!"

Ironically, the king of the new Oakland drug dealers that Brown writes about was Felix Mitchell. He and New York's Mr. "Untouchable,"Nicki Barnes, were the drug lords that the villain in my film *New Jack City* was based on. Was *Panther* in some way almost the prequel to *New Jack*? With the massive new influx of drugs, Felix Mitchell and Nicki Barnes were able to do for coke what Ford did to the auto plant industry. Could drug dealers of this stature even exist without the cooperation of authorities?

The minute you accept the fact that there are no poppy fields to make dope from in the ghetto, you have to ask where all this dope comes from. The minute that you accept the fact that there are no gun manufacturing plants in the ghetto, you have to ask where all these weapons come from. You'll never see a black gangster dropping dope out of his customized Cadillac helicopter into the ghetto below. Black gangsters don't make dope or guns, although they go to jail for it. There is sim-

The Alameda County Courthouse or "Moby Dick," as Huey called it, was another actual historical location. It had hardly changed at all from the late 1960s, when Huey was locked down inside. Our decorators had no building and minimal dressing to do setwise. On this spectacular day, we had several ex-Panthers coaching our Oakland extras and core actors through the marching and chanting of "Free Huey." Several of our diehard core L.A. Panther extras were so motivated that they drove themselves up from L.A. to join us voluntarily. For the actors and extras, most of us too young to have been Panthers, it was a time to live just a fraction of a movement that we missed. For the Panthers themselves, it was an almost surreal flashback, one that moved many of them emotionally. The BPP had incredible multiracial support—the Brown Berets (Hispanics); the Red Peril (Asians); the radical left, and, yes, even a group called "Honkies for Huey!" On that day under the brilliant Oakland sun, there seemed to be no racial, sexual, or generation gaps. We were all there representing "All Power to the People" in full force!

ply no logistical way that these large quantities of narcotics and weapons can get into all our major urban communities without the cooperation of authorities somewhere.

I worked briefly as a counselor in a Harlem drug rehab center in the late 1970s. But it was later, during my research for *New Jack City* that I gained exposure to New York's drug underground. I interviewed ex-dealers who had dealt for cops, ex-cops who supplied and admitted forcing some "qualified" addicts to deal with the threat of getting busted for noncooperation. I also talked with addicts, most of whom felt the "Just Say No" campaign was a sad publicity stunt. Uptown, whole blocks were dedicated to the crack trade. Dealers plied their wares in broad daylight, while terrified citizens cowered behind locked doors. Occasionally, the cops made a routine bust, but as long as the epidemic stayed above 125th Street, it was allowed to fester. One dealer pointed out that the stiff, new drug laws are used to crack heads of nonconnected, low-level minority dealers, while authorities consistently avoid busting the big traffickers.

A well documented case of this involves the Panamanian General Manuel Noriega. The CIA was forced to admit it paid Noriega some $320,000 while he was working with the U.S. Drug Enforcement Administration, supposedly to arrest drug smugglers. Even though Noriega himself was a known narcotics trafficker. On April 9, 1992 he was found guilty of cocaine and marijuana trafficking, racketeering, and money laundering. As the *New York Times* pointed out: "During the trial, ruling on national security grounds, the judge prohibited the defense from presenting evidence that it said would have shown that General Noriega was cooperating with the Central Intelligence Agency and the Defense Department when he committed some of the offenses."

I, in no way, mean to indict authorities or officers of the law across the board. It was a cop, disgusted by the narcotics plague in minority communities, who said, "Our current drug policy is aimed at the symptom while deliberately avoiding the cause."

Stokeley Carmichael astutely points out that America has historically reserved "special" treatment for Third World people. The extermi-

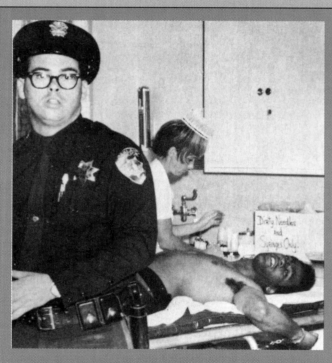 

Huey Newton in *Revolutionary Suicide* describes how police officers handcuffed him to a gurney and beat him after he had been critically wounded in the abdomen. When he spat blood on them, they covered his face with a towel, and beat him some more. Huey wrote that a young Dr. Thomas Finch committed reactionary suicide after Huey's first trial. His conscience would give him no peace after his treatment of Huey in the emergency room. The officer above is not known to have beaten Huey. Studies have shown that the more a police force reflects, racially and geographically, the group it polices, the less likely it is to develop an occupied army—us versus them—mentality. At the time, Oakland's mostly black community was policed by a

racist, almost entirely white police force that seemed more likely to "patrol and control" than to "protect and serve." *Panther* will undoubtedly be criticized by the dominant culture for showing these officers in such harsh light. But showing the nice cops in these instances would be like showing nice Nazis herding Jews into concentration camps. As ex-Panther leader David Hilliard points out, "The cops we dealt with were like the ones that beat Rodney King. Unfortunately, that was the reality. I'm sure there were good cops, but at the time, we didn't hear from them." In spite of that reality, Joe Don Baker plays a composite good cop in the movie, and our composite black FBI collaborator is a bad cop. Good and evil do not follow color lines.

nation of the red man, the enslavement of the black man, the atom bombing of the yellow man, and the dumping of toxic pesticides on the brown man are just a few examples of America's "legal" treatment of nonwhite people. The ghetto, the inner city is considered a Third World country within a country, and as such it is fair game.

Mao said that revolution comes from the barrel of a gun. Ironic that the guns the Panthers once held as symbols are now in the hands of young newly made gangsters and are used to kill each other. Ironic that drugs like coke, which became hip during the 1960s would one day pacify the movement. When you're on crack, you don't vote, you don't think politically, and you don't join the Black Panthers.

The BPP power base was medicated; the rise in militancy abated. There were no more uprisings after 1968 until the L.A. uprising in 1993, when the jury acquitted the police officers who brutalized Rodney King.

MAGIC HOUR

It's magic hour in the community, the sun is setting, our camera cranes up over the intersection of 55th and Market, where the Panthers once years ago rallied for that stoplight. It's now 1995.

The voices of political leaders have been replaced by rappers boasting from a passing boom box about a life rife with guns, drugs, and money. It's everywhere, the yuppie materialistic "me first" mentality, shamelessly represented in ghetto gold by those who don't understand. It's the end of the film. Judge's voice, older now, explains that:

"The authorities allowed the drugs to flood the black community, but the drugs overflowed the borders of the ghetto and ended up on all America's doorstep.... In 1970 there were some three hundred thousand addicts. Today there are over three million. The way I see it the struggle continues."

The struggle will continue. No doubt there will be paranoia about this movie inciting violence. You could see that coming a mile away, even though there have been no unfortunate incidents with other African American historical pieces such as *Malcolm X* or *Posse*.

When I sat through our second test screening, the one for the so-

In keeping with the "Power to the People" theme, composer Stanley Clarke kept the score organic and human, even during the big epic scenes. The film starts with the voice of demonstrators singing "We Shall Overcome" faintly, tentatively, yet full of hope. As the film builds, the music evolves to full orchestra. Jazz tends to have a cool sound, and when used in cinema often distances you from the characters. Rather than go with the expected cool-funk electronic sound, I wanted a classical, natural score to ennoble the movement. Stanley, who is versed in everything from jazz to funk to classical, was able to capture the historical moments in musical form. The human heart beats at some sixty times a minute. Most of our music was recorded from fifty-nine to sixty-two beats a minute. Stanley points out that the chords he used in the *Panther* themes were similar to those used in church hymns. Not only would the music be based on the beating of the human heart, but it would have a strong, emotional resonance.

Panther has two sountracks, a rap awareness record and an actual film soundtrack. Money from both albums was donated to the Dr. Huey P. Newton Foundation and the Committee to Free Ex-Panther Geronimo Pratt.

Above: **S**tanley Clarke
In background: Kadeem Hardison as Judge talks about joining the Black Panthers with Tyrin Turner playing Cy.

called "core demographic" (that's studioese for boys from the hood), something interesting happened. The crowd went in there pumped and got crazy vocal, as you'd expect, during the confrontational militant scenes. As the movie progressed, the Panthers suggest exercising their legal rights to arm themselves and defend themselves. Overhearing this, an old jailbird (played by my dad) cackles that if black folks ever got guns they'd be stupid enough to shoot each other. This spoke directly to the, now subdued audience.

When the brother working with the FBI appeared in the film —representing the numerous black informants the FBI had on its payroll—the audience again got quiet. (Roger Smith was incredibly brave not only to play this role but to play it well.) Good and evil don't simplistically fall along color lines. After all, if there is no enemy within, the enemy without can do no harm. In the third act, the mobster kicks the facts about the narcotics and the devastating effect it will have on the black community. The kids, some of whom sling rocks (deal drugs), got so quiet, you could hear a rat pissing on cotton. No one moved. Did they hate the damn movie? Should I start seeking new employment? I glanced over at Pop, then to Preston.

Nope, no one knows the deal, nothing to do but chill and wait. A nervous assistant ushered me out of the theater before the picture ended so the audience wouldn't recognize me and perhaps affect the test scores. I wanted desperately to catch their reactions, but no go.

Fifteen minutes later, and I'm like an expectant father, trying not to stand over some accountant type as he tallies up the test scores. He seems perplexed and starts over, damn. "Is there a problem?" I ask, annoyed, that I'm getting annoyed and getting more so. "I'm not sure," he replies, flustered as he recalculates the numbers yet again. His boss or associate or whatever this guy is comes hustling over. They whisper in hushed tones together, and I wonder if Scorsese or De Palma have to test their movies with the core Italian demographic. I know they don't, but wondering this kind of crap helps pass the time while you try not to think about the scores.

"You got a 98," the accountant says finally in disbelief. "What's that mean?" someone asks. "It means the numbers are hallucinogenic," boomed Peter Graves, the resident guru of marketing from Polygram. "You don't get numbers like this. These are terrific," he exclaimed, slapping me a victorious five. Peter had reason to celebrate. As a supporter of this project from the beginning, his balls were in the sand on this one, too. "It's all in the writing," Pops said as we hugged, relieved as hell. "Yeah, but the directing really makes the film," I added.

Later I called Tim Bevan and Eric Fellner of Working Title, our partner company, and of course "Big Cheese" Brit Michael Kuhn, who was key in getting the financing, to share the good news. Their response was to ask in that dry British way, "What bloody film did you show them?"

In the final analysis, of course, all these numbers really mean is that for whatever reason, that night, in that theater, those 457 teenagers dug the movie.

Far from being a call to arms, they saw it as a call to consciousness. A call to reexamine what we were all doing or not doing, not to point a finger or much less a gun at anyone.

For me…that night was cool. Whether the thing makes money or not, someone out there got it.

A black South African pointed out to me that when we hear of Africa, we hear of starvation and apartheid. When we hear of Bosnia, we hear about the horrors of ethnic cleansing. And when we hear from African American filmmakers, we hear of the pain and suffering in the ghettos. He said, "We all hear each other's pain. What will you show us when you've already shown us the hood and its pain?"

My answer would be "hope," a way out. A story about a couple of young men and women who read some laws, formed an organization, and showed us a way out. Not the only way, not even necessarily the best way, but a way out nonetheless.

Someone once said you have two loves in your life. What you do, and who you do it with. Well, I couldn't have asked for more. I was fortunate enough to take on a project I believed in and work with folks I cared about—especially the old filmmaker who showed me how to climb the mountain.

In this lifetime, while we were both alive and had our health, we did it. I suppose I'd add one more "love" to those first two. And that is the love of being able to say a little something or do a little something that improves this place before we leave it.

Working with my father at this level was a dream come true. People are often surprised that we can artistically agree and disagree without jeopardizing our mutual trust. He is my best friend; he is also a different filmmaker with his own cinematic approach to accomplishing the same agenda. My dad had lived and fought the same ideological battles alongside the Panthers. He often assumed that the audience would know as much about the politics of the times as he did. I, on the other hand, felt that the movie should be accessible and enjoyable to someone who knew nothing and cared nothing about the politics. Ultimately, it was a better movie for having two fathers.

DICK GREGORY COMMENTS ON *PANTHER*

I got a call from Melvin Van Peebles about being a part of his upcoming film, *Panther.* I told Melvin that I've never had any interest in doing movies. I've got ten children, five grandchildren and I am very, very careful about what I do that will affect the young minds of America. Particularly black folks, particularly women! I also told him that I didn't want to be a part of anything that would glamorize filth. But Melvin Van Peebles has integrity. When it comes to people in the movie industry that I trust, the names are Melvin Van Peebles, Melvin Van Peebles, and Melvin Van Peebles. Melvin and his son Mario created an entertaining movie, and I am proud to be a part of it. It's Melvin's everyday walk of life. He talks the way prophets talk, and it's that love that Martin Luther King, Jr. talked about. When Melvin talks about the system, racism, prejudice and segregation, there's no hate there; it's facts! I see this film as a new Bible. To say, here's the way, when you're talking about telling it like it is.

I realized one day that people were not only controlled by drugs and alcohol; but they also are controlled by food and nutrition. And the Black Panthers were smart enough to discover this. You can never really understand hunger until you understand the politics of hunger. So what the world will see from this movie is actually the politics of America. And what the establishment did was portray the Panthers as a militant hate group in an attempt to make the world think that what the Panthers got in trouble for was calling cops pigs or for talking about killing cops. What they **really** got in trouble for was creating and organizing simple feeding and health care programs in the black community.

The politics of America was represented by J. Edgar Hoover, the FBI, and don't think for one minute that the CIA wasn't also involved. In trying to help young babies and their own community, the Panthers were misrepresented, wiped out, and murdered for simply teaching their own people to take control of their lives.

Before I did the movie, I didn't know Mario. When I met him, I met a kind man. With Mario, there's no arrogance, there's no insecurity in the way he smiles and the way he directs. I don't know that much about the people who were performing, but you knew there were no drugs or ego problems on the set. Once I got there and looked at the script, I liked it. I began to feel Mario. The professionalism demonstrated on the set was extraordinary. Wherever you were supposed to be, someone was right there to come and get you and take you to the next location. I'd never met any of the actors or crew, but under Mario's direction, we worked as a family. When we broke for dinner, you didn't see Melvin or Mario with special food. I never saw one group of people eating in one place and others in another place. We were all together. On the set everyone

was treated well, and that's what you see on the screen.

This movie is not a documentary. It's entertaining, it's enjoyable, it's historical, and it puts you right there. The women in this movie were treated as equal and clean. Women in films today often are used as sex objects, but not in this movie. What you will see in this movie are women who fought in the struggle for their rights as well as the rights of the black community. Most movies of this nature never really tell the story in a way that puts you there with the characters, seeing what they see, feeling what they feel. I see this film as the first type of movie that could be and should be a guideline for all other groups of people to follow to tell their own stories.

When I'm asked who the Panthers are, my description is this. If the *Panthers* were a group that were talking about your civic duties—pay your taxes, the white Christian work ethnic, join the army, be good citizens—we wouldn't know about them. The Panthers were talking about taking care of the downtrodden. Love your neighbors as you love yourselves. They were willing to die and they died for their rights, as well as the rights of their community—black sisters and brothers. The Panthers were an extension of Martin Luther King, Jr.., SNCC, Malcolm X, the NAACP, the Urban League, Elijah Muhammad, and the Black Movement in general. The Panthers said, **"THIS IS OUR RIGHT, THIS IS THE LAW!"** This is what America goes to war for—to protect the rights. That's all the Panthers were doing—going by the laws. But then the government said, we're going to do two things: first we're going to change the laws; then we're going to destroy the Panthers (which they did). Then we're going to see to it that their community will never be focused again. So they brought the drugs in. They neutralized the community with drugs, unemployment, and overcrowded conditions.

We know now that the whole drug culture was to neutralize the people. But we don't know how many people, ministers, business people, and ordinary citizens were framed by this government at the time when nobody looked at the FBI as anything but sitting at the right hand of God. We know what happened to the Black Panther Party, but we don't know about all those thousands of people and thousands of organizations that were disgraced. People went to their graves believing that their loved ones were involved in certain things just don't happen.

The Panthers were not a Peace Corps run by the government that said go in and clean up the neighborhood....Cut the grass and paint the picket fences. The Panthers weren't interested in the physical appearance of the black community. But they were interested in the soul of the black community. The Panthers knew that once they took care of the human needs of the people, the picket fence would be taken care of.

From *Panther* we see the Panther Party as they were.

I think this movie is the continuation of The Movement, and now we have in this movie the Document, the Bible of the Movement.

—*Dick Gregory*

Almost from the day the Black Panther Party was founded in 1966, the police, and the FBI in particular, have been trying to rewrite the Party's history. On the whole, they have been very successful at creating an image of the Party as a bunch of thugs and thieves cloaking criminal conspiracies behind revolutionary rhetoric. Actually, the Black Panther Party was a political movement, a mass movement, a community organization dedicated to the revolutionary idea of ending oppression and returning control of our communities to our communities.

We understood that oppression cut across color and class lines; it was all economic and it was all political. We organized based on that. We didn't care what color you were. So we had coalitions with the Latinos, with the Asians, and with revolutionary organizations the world over. Our focus was on the politics of humanism. But you would never know any of this if all you knew about the Black Panther Party was what you read in newspapers or saw on television.

You would never know about our community service programs, which we called survival programs. We had free health clinics and free food programs. We gave away more than twenty thousand bags of groceries. We escorted senior citizens to the bank and back when they cashed their checks. We had testing programs for various diseases such as lead poisoning and sickle cell anemia. We had housing programs. That's why we existed, not because of our rhetoric, not because of the guns. It was about our service to the community.

The press keyed into the guns because it was sensational. But the Black Panther Party did not have the police, or fighting the police, as its primary focus. We Had a ten-point program. Point no. 7 addressed the BPP and its self-defense policy against the police. But before No. 7 we talked about employment, housing, medical care. Our politics of self-defense came way down the list. The guns were really a strategic action, a symbolic gesture used for political and educational purposes. That whole Sacramento demonstration was to let people know that laws were being legislated to disarm the black community, not just the Panthers. We did not see ourselves as separate from the community. Yes, we had guns. We had a right to those guns—both a constitutional right and a right under California state law—and we don't apologize for it. We were not lawbreakers. Those guns were there for self-defense.

But the self-defense we were really concerned with was self-defense against hunger, inadequate housing, inferior health care. The guns were used very effectively by the press and the FBI to put us into a very negative box.

In the past few years, however, we have begun to reclaim the image of the Panthers and to restore our reputation by telling the truth about the Black Panther Party. My book, *This Side of Glory,* and former Party Chair Elaine Brown's book, *A Taste of Power,* have given us a new and more positive standing in society. One recent book, *Shadow of the Panther,* by Hugh Pearson, chose to ignore the FBI's well documented effort to destroy the Party and Huey in particular and to rely on testimony admitted by agents and informants. Huey's addiction was a 1970s phenomenon anyway. The Party started in 1966. To take one individual, even Huey, at one point in his life, and by using deliberate disinformation portray him as the whole of an organization that existed all over the country and internationally does severe damage to the Party, not to mention to the credibility of the author.

The FBI has always attempted to criminalize the Black Panther Party, to make us seem like anything except a genuine political movement in this country. If they could call us criminals, they would treat us like criminals and go after us like criminals, regardless of the facts.

That's why another effort that Elaine and I are involved in through the Dr. Huey P. Newton Foundation is so important. In partnership with the Oakland Museum, we are organizing an archival exhibit of the Black Panther Party that will travel all over the world. All our history will be there. All of our newspapers, writings, film footage, tape recordings, manuscripts, FBI documents, Panther posters, and some 300 photographs. For those people who want to know what we were really about, they can see it for themselves.

And that's why Mario and Melvin's *Panther* is so important as well, because it does show the Party's survival programs as well as the government's war on us. It's quite appropriate that Mario and Melvin made this movie, because Huey Newton, the leader and founder of the Party, had much respect for Melvin as a filmmaker. He especially was impressed by Melvin's movie, *Sweet Sweetback's Baadasssss Song.* We thought Melvin was a great and very revolutionary filmmaker. As a matter of fact, Huey wrote an analytical piece about the movie called, "He Won't Bleed Me: A Revolutionary Analysis of 'Sweet Sweeback's Badasssss Song'," which appeared in the special issue of the Panther newspaper and also in Huey's book, *To Die for the People.*

All of the *Panther* members—all chapters—were directed to go see this movie, because Huey saw in it a very strong revolutionary theme. Huey saw Melvin as a pioneer for young filmmakers like his son Mario, John Singleton, the Hudlin brothers, and the Hughes brothers. People like Melvin Van Peebles really opened the door for the black filmmakers of today by taking what we consider to be a very radical departure from the traditional black films.

I hope Melvin and Mario's film will whet the appetite of the youth and that they will hunger to know more about the youth movement called the Black Panther Party. I hope that *Panther* will serve as a catalyst for today's youth—black, white, Latino, Asian, women—and will spur them to create new movements challenging the powers responsible for the degrading and decaying conditions permeating our communities across America. We need these movements today as desperately as we did in 1966.

Huey said *Sweet Sweetback* put forth the ideas of what we must do to build unity in our community. He said we should see the film often and learn as much as we could from it. If he were alive today, Huey would say the same thing about *Panther.*

—David Hilliard

I still have vivid memories of the day in June 1971 when some friends and I stuffed ourselves into one of the guys' car to make the short drive from Princeton University to New Brunswick, New Jersey, the closest town to show Melvin Van Peebles' *Sweet Sweetback's Baadasssss Song*. Neither my life nor black cinema would ever be the same from then on.

Sweetback showed Hollywood that there was a potential gold mine in films for a black audience. To black Americans starved for images of ourselves on screen that had dignity, courage, arrogance, and balls it provided a glimpse of what was possible. We responded in record numbers. And to aspiring black filmmakers, it showed the way and in doing so spawned a rebirth of black cinema that has continued to grow, albeit in fits and starts.

For me, *Sweetback* marked the beginning of a relationship with Melvin, that led to one with Mario and *Panther*—the two together standing as a high point of my career.

Shortly after the release of *Posse*, my second film with Mario (*New Jack City* was the first), I returned to New York to work with Spike Lee on *Crooklyn*. During early preproduction, I was approached by Melvin and Mario about working with them on a film about the Black Panther Party to be based on a novel by Melvin. I immediately said yes. I had wanted to do a film about the Panthers for

a long time. As a child of the tumultuous 1960s, I came of age with the BBP. Huey, Bobby, David, Eldridge, Kathleen, and Fred Hampton were heroes of mine.

The problem was that preproduction on *Panther* was slated to start immediately. I had never before left a film before finishing, and I certainly did not want to burn a bridge with Spike, but I badly wanted to do this picture.

Back in 1968, as Bobby and Huey were building the Party in Oakland, I was deciding to go after a career in film business and dreaming of one day making a film about them. I owed those brothers big time for helping keep me from Vietnam.

In summer 1969, I was summoned by Uncle Sam to come to the Kansas City Selective Service office for my physical in preparation for being drafted and shipped to Nam. As far as I was concerned, there were few fates worse than that, so I panicked. I knew that I would pass the physical, and I started thinking about escape to Canada. Just as I was about to give up hope, the other draftees and I were instructed to complete a form that requested information about membership in the Communist Party, the John Birch Society, or "other subversive organizations." I checked "other" and indicated that I was a member of the Black Panther Party, Trenton chapter.

All hell broke loose. I was ushered swiftly to an

upstairs conference room, where I was joined by stern-looking fellows who identified themselves as members of U.S. Army Intelligence. They broke out notepads, started a tape recorder, and grilled me on the nature and extent of my involvement with the Panthers. Although I was certainly a Panther sympathizer, I was never a member and eventually told them this.

A few days later I arrived home early one morning after partying all night to find two FBI agents on the front porch, talking to my mother. They had been asking about my friends and associates. They interrogated me about my political views and eventually asked if I would consider trying to assassinate President Nixon. A few days after that, I received in the mail a rejection slip from the army on the basis that I was a security risk. Such was the nature of the paranoia in this country about political activism, militancy, communism, and the Black Panther Party.

Of, course, the other hallmark of the 1960s was the drug culture. Till I reached high school in Kansas City in 1964, alcohol was the only drug my peers and I had any interest in. At the same time, political activism in the black community was at a high point. By the time I left for college, even in Kansas City it involved schools, churches, community organizations of all kinds. The community was on the move.

By the time I returned from Princeton after my freshman year, however, things were changing rapidly. Drugs of every kind were becoming commonplace. Guys I once cruised with guzzling wine were heavily into marijuana and hashish and soon heroin and cocaine. Back at Princeton, the same thing was happening, but the drugs of choice—marijuana, acid, mescaline—were not addictive.

Looking back, I am reminded of a New York Police Department inspector in the South Bronx who in an interview in Brent Owens' documentary, "A Cry for Help," talks about the critical importance of drugs and alcohol in helping him do his job. "I'd hate to see what would happen here if so many of these young people were not permanently narcotized." It's difficult to think of these developments as coincidence.

I went to Spike to ask to leave *Crooklyn*, even though I loved that project as well. When I'd first read the script, it brought tears to my eyes. Even though I had a long and rewarding history with Spike going back to *Do the Right Thing*, I think because of his own respect for the Van Peebles and the Panther legacy and my strong desire to do it, he agreed.

The making of *Panther* was more challenging and rewarding than I could have imagined. After arriving in L.A., the first order of business was to develop the budget and schedule with the production manager, Brent Owens. Based on our mutual experience on many films, including *Malcolm X*, we had a good handle on what would be required to do such a picture. We would not be able to bet anywhere the kind of money we had for "X," but we decided we could do justice to the subject with $10-15 million.

When we presented the initial budget of approxi-mately $12 million, we figured we'd be asked to cut another million or so. But we were prepared to argue that issue. We were totally unprepared when we were told the film would probably not be "green lit" unless it could be brought in for a little more than half that amount.

The next few months were a frustrating series of meetings, debates, arguments, and pleading. Ultimately, Mario, Melvin, and I decided we wanted to make this film a reality badly enough that we would make any sacrifices to bring it about. We started by volunteering to reduce our respective fees drastically. All the cast agreed to work for what was in many cases far below their quotes. We also reluctantly decided to shoot most of the film in L.A., not the Bay area, to save on travel and living costs and to cram filming into an almost impossible forty-day shooting schedule.

By hook and crook, we chiseled the budget down to a dangerously low but acceptable level, but that was not the only hurdle. The prevailing wisdom in the industry regarding black films is that if a film appeals to black youth, it will be successful, and it not, it won't. There was real doubt about whether young people had any interest in seeing a movie about events that happened twenty-five years ago.

The distribution company decided to have a black marketing firm do focus group research with young (16-19 year-old) inner-city blacks to determine their awareness of and interest in the Black Panthers. As Ivan Jusang of MEE Productions began to make his report, my heart sank. We were certainly dead in the water. I watched in horror as on videotape the youngsters—chosen because they were representative of the style/trend setters in the black community—were read a list of names and told to indicate by a show of hands the names they recognized. Huey Newton, Bobby Seale, Eldridge Cleaver, Stokeley Carmichael, H. Rap Brown. Not a single hand went up. Worse yet, finally one young man timidly but seriously volunteered: "Huey Newton. Ain't he a cookie?"

The presentation continued, however. Now we listened to these same kids after they'd been shown footage of the Panthers from "Eyes on the Prize" and other sources. They were excited, inspired, and angered—angry that knowledge of these Black Panthers had not been passed on to them. Some vowed to insist that the Panthers be covered in their curriculums.

Ivan ended his presentation with a raw, homegrown music video that these same young people were moved to produce about the Panthers. We were vindicated. The film was finally green lit ten months after I'd ask Spike if I could leave *Crooklyn*.

Now the real work was to begin. As tough as things sometimes were, over the next few months I couldn't help but feel a sense of privilege to be one of the few people in the world who actually gets a chance to fulfill his dreams.

BLACK PANTHER PARTY
A CHRONOLOGY

1965

August 6

-The Voting Rights Act, prohibiting literacy tests and requiring federally appointed registrars, becomes law.

August 11–16

-Rebellion in Watts, a predominantly black district of Los Angeles, California, leaves 35 dead, 1,000 injured, 4,000 arrested, and an estimated $40 million damage.

August

-Lowdes County Freedom Organization, an independent political party in rural Mississippi, adopts the symbol of the black panther for its organization.

-Huey Newton's mentor, Donald Warden, creates Economic Night in a storefront located next door to the future BPP office on Grove Street. He also organizes Soul Students Advisory Council.

1966

March 17

-In Berkeley, California, local police interrupt an impromptu street corner recitation of the poem "Uncle Sammy Call Me Full of Lucifer," resulting in an altercation and arrest of Bobby Seale, Huey P. Newton, and Weasel (Gerald Horton, aka Rafeeq Naji). Charges are later dismissed.

March 29

-Oakland, California, police officer shoots a black man, accused of trespassing, 7 times in the back; he is left paralyzed.

-San Francisco, California, police officer shoots Matthew Johnson, a 16-year-old car theft suspect, to death in Hunter's Point.

May 5

-Citizens demonstrate and rally at Oakland police station and courthouse to protest the jailing of Mark Comfort, candidate for 15th Assembly District. Comfort was convicted for failing to disperse at the scene of a nonviolent demonstration against the racist hiring practices of the *Oakland Tribune*.

May 26

-The United Employers (all white men) support Oakland's City Council by voting in opposition to the formation of a citizen review board to oversee activities of the Oakland police department.

June/July

-In Oakland, Curtis Baker addresses the California Advisory Commission of the U.S. Civil Rights Commission on police-community relations. Baker, representing local citizens, called for a civilian police review board.

-Oakland's Bay Area Rapid Transit forces black citizens to sell homes to make way for ground transit, creating a major housing crisis. Justice on BART organized in protest.

-Forty-three United States cities go up in smoke, including Washington, D.C., Baltimore, Atlanta, and Detroit, leaving 7 dead and 3,500 arrested.

-Citizens in the Fillmore district of San Francisco riot in reaction to police violence.

-In San Francisco 500 people gather at City Hall to protest arrest of sit-in demonstrators in 1964 at the Sheraton-Palace Hotel.

-Donald Warden, organizer of Oakland's Afro-American Association, demands the implementation of Black Studies curriculum and protests the draft.

-Bobby Seale is employed at the federally funded Anti-poverty Program at 55th and Market Streets in Oakland.

-The Afro-American Association Center opens at 42nd and Grove Streets, employing youth mentors and sponsoring study groups and cultural activities. Huey Newton's mentors, Fritz Pointer and Dave Patterson, serve as co-directors of the center.

-In Oakland Congress of Racial Equality (CORE) initiates a fair hiring policy. They circulate lists of business participants and a boycott list of those who refuse.

August

-In Watts, California, the Negro Citizen Alert Patrol cruises South Central Los Angeles in radio-equipped cars, monitoring police radio calls and observing police conduct. Their vehicles are marked "To Protect and Serve."

-Elijah Turner, chairman of the Ad Hoc Committee for Quality Education, leads picket line of Oakland school board requesting free hot lunches for schoolchildren.

September

-Students at Oakland Technical High School organize Black Student Union (BSU).

-A black car theft suspect is shot to death in Hunter's Point. The youth was an unarmed teenager.

-The black students at Merritt College propose Black Studies curriculum and demand a black person be hired to administer the program.

October 15

-Huey P. Newton and Bobby Seale write the first draft of the Black Panther Party for Self-Defense (BPP) 10-point program.

-Newton and Seale immediately applied point No. 7: "We want an immediate end to the police brutality and murder of black people."

November

-The BPP receives its first donation, from Japanese American revolutionary, Richard Aoki, an M-1 and a 9mm gun.

December

-Eldridge Cleaver is released from Folsom Prison, paroled in San Francisco, and joins *Ramparts* magazine as a staff writer. Bob Avakian is the magazine's research editor.

-Sixteen-year-old Bobby Hutton becomes the first male recruit of the BPP.

1967

January

-First BPP office opens at 5624 Grove Street, Oakland, California.

-Chairman Mao Zedong's *Quotations* is sold in front of the University of California, Berkeley, Sather's Gate, to raise money to support the BPP.

-Panthers patrol the streets of Oakland.

-Kenny Freeman and Roy Ballard organize the Black Panther Party of Northern California in San Francisco, California.

February

-Local police confront armed Panthers coming out of Grove Street BPP office. However, the Panther guns are unloaded in compliance with California gun law; thus the Oakland police department backs down after a verbal confrontation.

-The BPP of Northern California (San Francisco) invite the BPP for Self-Defense (Oakland) to join them in providing security for Betty Shabazz, widow of Malcolm X, at the First Annual Malcolm X Grassroots Memorial at Hunter's Point.

February 21

-The Panthers escort Betty Shabazz from the San Francisco airport to *Ramparts* for an interview with Eldridge Cleaver. A rift is created between the San Francisco Panthers and the Oakland Panthers primarily because of this incident.

April 1
-In Richmond, California, Denzil Dowell is shot and killed by sheriff's deputies at Third and Chestly, an unincorporated area of North Richmond. Panthers respond to request from the Dowell family for protection from police harassment.

April 15
-In New York City, at the United Nations, the Black United Front organizes demonstration and rally against Vietnam War.

April 18
-In Pittsburg, California, black citizens and police exchange gunfire.

April 25
-The first issue of the *Black Panther Party: Black Community News Service* is published. This four-page mimeograph newspaper headlines "Why Was Denzil Dowell Killed?"

May 2
-Thirty armed Panthers and their supporters go to the California state capitol at Sacramento to protest the Mulford Act, a bill aimed at banning the display of loaded weapons.

May 15
The Black Panther details what happened in Sacramento. The newspaper also includes local news, the BPP's 10-point program, Pocket Lawyer of Legal First Aid, and subscription advertisement.

May 22
-Huey Newton responds to a citizen's complaint that the Oakland police department entered a neighborhood home without a warrant or provocation. Newton was arrested after ordering the police to leave. When Bobby Seale went to bail Huey Newton out he was arrested under an 1887 law barring possession of a gun near a jail.

June
-Huey Newton issues Executive Mandate No. 2, officially drafting Stokeley Carmichael as Black Panther Party field marshal for the East Coast.

-The Office of Economic Opportunity/Community Complaints receives petition for traffic signal at 55th and Market, where 3 children were killed by cars and 7 injured. The Panthers act as crossing guards, and their presence speeds up date on construction of stoplight.

-Riots explode in major cities, including Newark, Cleveland, and Detroit.

-In Los Angeles the police department raid the Nation of Islam mosque.

July
-In Hunter's Point Bobby Seale addresses more than 200 black youths on politics.

-Assemblyman Don Mulford's act to ban loaded weapons passes the California legislature.

August 1
-The construction work on the stoplight at 55th and Market Streets begins.

-J. Edgar Hoover's FBI directs its counterintelligence program (COINTELPRO) to "neutralize" and "destroy any attempts of a Messiah rising amongst them." Hoover starts the FBI's "Rabble-Rouser Index."

September
-BSUs organized at local high school campuses become more visible and vocal. BSU demands include receiving the same status as other campus organizations. Many early Panther recruits came from Oakland Technical High School BSU.

-Cultural awareness programs center around the Merritt College campus as well as the Cultural Center located south of the Afro-American campus.

October 7
-Stop the Draft Week in Oakland begins with a mass rally and march at UC Berkeley and ends at Oakland's Army Recruitment Center at 14th and Clay.
-Huey Newton and David Hilliard as well as writers for *The Black Panther* attend the demonstrations.

October 27
-Huey Newton attends a party celebrating an end to his probation, at the Afro-American Cultural Center at 42nd and Grove Streets.
-In Meridian, Mississippi, seven, including a deputy sheriff and Ku Klux Klan leader, are convicted in the murders of civil rights workers James Chaney, Michael Schwerner, and Andrew Goodman.

October 28
-At 4:56 A.M. Oakland officer John Frey is killed and officer Herbert Haines wounded in a predawn altercation after stopping Huey Newton and Gene McKinney. Newton is also critically wounded.

November
-San Francisco attorney Charles Garry, a long time advocate for social justice, is chosen by the Party to represent Huey Newton.

November 13
-In Oakland, the Alameda County grand jury indicts Huey Newton on charges of first-degree murder, attempted murder, and kidnapping.

December
The Black Panther increases its circulation tenfold.

1968

January
-The Southern California branch of the BPP is organized by Alprentice "Bunchy" Carter, deputy minister of defense for Southern California. The BPP office is at Central

Avenue and 43rd street.

January 15
-National captain David Hilliard is arrested while passing out BPP leaflets at Oakland Technical High School.

January 16
-At 3:30 A.M. San Francisco police officers break down the apartment door of Eldridge and Kathleen Cleaver. The officers ransack the apartment without a search warrant. Emory Douglas is also present.

February 8
-In Orangeburg, South Carolina, on the campus of South Carolina State College, local police backed by the National Guard fire on a crowd of unarmed students; 33 black activists are shot, and three die.

February 17
-A "Free Huey" Newton rally is held at the Oakland Auditorium on Newton's birthday. More than 5,000 supporters attend including Stokeley Carmichael, H. Rap Brown, James Forman, Ron Dellums, and Peace and Freedom Party representatives.

February 18
-A "Free Huey" Newton rally takes place in Southern California.

February 25
-At 2:00A.M. Berkeley police officers break down the door and ransack the home of Bobby and Artie Seale. The Seales are charged with conspiracy to commit murder. Charges are later dropped for lack of evidence.

-After leaving the Seales' home, Bunchy Carter, Anthony Coltrale, Audrey Hudson, and David Hilliard are arrested and charged with carrying a concealed weapon.

February 26
-The BPP holds a press conference damning the arrests and blatant harassment of Panthers by local police in an attempt to drain the BPP treasury.

March
-Arthur (Glen) Morris, brother of Bunchy Carter, is shot and killed by "agents of the U.S. government." He is the first member of the BPP to be killed.

-Anthony Coltrale is killed in Watts by a local police officer.

-The Kansas City BPP office is raided by police, and 5 Panthers are arrested.

-Huey Newton issues Executive Mandate No. 4 from jail.

March 4
-An FBI memo from J. Edgar Hoover outlines goals to his staff to "Prevent the coalition of militant black nationalist groups. In unity there is strength…black nationalist groups might be the first step toward a real Mau Mau. Prevent the rise of a black Messiah who would unify and electrify the black nationalist movement."

March 16
-At a conference sponsored by the Peace and Freedom Party (PFP) in Richmond, California, the organization announces its coalition with the BPP. The PFP slate includes Party members. Kathleen Cleaver is elected to run for the San Francisco 18th Assembly District and Bobby Seale for Oakland's 17th Assembly District. The PFP donates $3,000 to the Huey Newton Defense Fund.

April
-The New York BPP chapter is organized.

April 3
-The Oakland police department raids Father Neil's church, where Party members are holding a meeting.

April 4
-Dr. Martin Luther King, Jr., assassinated at the Lorraine Motel, Memphis, Tennessee. Riots occur in major cities across the county, but Oakland remains calm due to the efforts of the BPP.

April 5
-The Los Angeles Police department raids the Student Nonviolent Coordinating Committee (SNCC) office while members attend a Martin Luther King, Jr., memorial service.

April 6
-An Oakland police shoot-out results in the murder of Bobby Hutton; Eldridge Cleaver is wounded. Seven other Panthers are arrested.

April 7
-Panther rally/potluck at Defermery Park in Oakland generates the largest turnout ever.

-Three Panthers are arrested in Seattle, Washington.

April 9
-Two Black Panther women are putting up posters announcing Party candidates for the PFP when twelve officers from Oakland, armed with shotguns, stop their vehicle and search it without probable cause.

-Oakland residents report seeing police officers tearing down PFP campaign posters.

-Panther volunteers register Oakland citizens to vote.

April 11
- A group called Blacks Strike for Justice organizes under the leadership of Paul Cobb, a member of the West Oakland Planning Committee. The group plans to strike at Oakland's establishment through its pocketbook. A boycott begins this day of absentee-owned businesses that have racist policies and hire no blacks.

April 13
-Funeral services for Bobby Hutton held at Ephesians Church of God in Christ on Alcatraz Avenue in Berkeley. More than 2,500 attend the funeral.

-A memorial rally for Hutton is held in front of the bullet-ridden scene of the crime, at 1218 28th Street.

-Four Panthers returning from Bobby Hutton's funeral are arrested on suspicion of robbery, at Grove and 21st streets.

April
-Paul Cobb arrested for interfering with an arrest after he asked a patrolman why ten police cars are crowded onto a single block.

-Eldridge Cleaver's parole is revoked without a hearing.

May
-Charles o Bursey, a political prisoner, is incarcerated nude in the infamous "hole" (concrete floor, hole in the floor, no running water, no toilet, no lights, no mattress, green mush for meals). He suffers seizures and is given no medical attention. Bursey dies years later from a head tumor.

May 4
- *The Black Panther* hits the street with headlines "Free All Black Political Prisoners, Eldridge," " Pigs Ambush Panthers," "Panthers Sue City of Oakland," "Pigs Use Mace in False Arrest," and "A Tribute to Lil Bobby."

May 10
-Panthers who were arrested in connection with the April 6 shoot-out call a press conference to repudiate confessions.

May 18
-The Oakland Seven are arraigned in Oakland for October 1967 antidraft demonstrations.

May 25
-Thirty-two arrested, including 4 professors, in connection with sit-in occupation of San Francisco State's Administration Building.

June
-San Francisco Party captain Dexter Woods arrested for curfew violation and given 5 days in jail.

June 8
-Bobby Seale is convicted of carrying a loaded shotgun near jail and is sentenced to 3 years' probation.

June 9
-At 9:00A.M. a "Free Huey" marathon at churches and Party offices begins throughout the Bay Area to mobilize mass support.

June 12
-Eldridge Cleaver is released from Vacaville prison (via judge writ of habeas corpus) by Superior Court Judge Sherwin.

June 25
-Eldridge Cleaver takes Panther case to United Nations.

June 30
-Berkeley mayor Wallace J. S. Johnson enacts a citywide curfew (from 8:00P.M. to 6:00A.M.) after a third night of rioting by antidraft protesters.

July

-The West Oakland Panther office opened by Tommy Jones, Glen Stafford, and other dedicated Panther volunteers.

-The Seattle BPP office is raided by local police.

-Captain Aaron Dixon of the Seattle BPP and Panther Curtis Harris are arrested for grand larceny. Both are eventually found not guilty.

-Captain Dexter Woods of the San Francisco BPP arrested for interference with police.

July 13
-Judge Friedman denies Huey Newton's motion to strike a prior conviction of assault with a deadly weapon. Huey had pleaded self-defense in the Odell Lee incident. Charles Garry goes to the State District Court of Appeal for a right to dismiss the prior conviction; it is denied.

July 15–16
-More than 6,000 protesters come out in support of Huey Newton on the steps of Alameda County Courthouse in Oakland. The national and international press is present as well as the National Guard.

-The newly formed Brown Berets make their appearance on the courthouse steps in support of Huey. They wear brown berets, khaki shirts, and brown pants.

July 17
-Huey Newton takes the stand for the first time in his own defense, but only to say that he is a pauper. Newton states that he has no money and cannot afford to have people flown from out of town to testify at his trial. The purpose of the testimony is to make it possible for Garry to submit two affidavits from eastern doctors stating that certain persons should not be allowed to serve on the jury.

July 18
-Attorney Charles Garry makes a motion that the jury for Huey's trial should be selected from his peers and that the current panel be dismissed.

July 27
-Eldridge Cleaver speaks at Syracuse University.

August
-The West Oakland Party office is raided and ransacked by police.

-In Newark, the Panther office is firebombed.

-In Detroit, Panthers and police have a shoot-out; however, there are no injuries.

-Five Seattle Panthers are harassed in their car by local police.

August 3
-At the PFP Convention in San Francisco, Eldridge Cleaver is elected as the presidential candidate.

August 5
-A Los Angeles shoot-out between police

and Panthers leaves 2 Panthers killed.

August 15
-David Hilliard, George Murray, and Landon Williams in Mexico City are prevented from traveling to Cuba.

August 16
-Chairman Bobby Seale and Captain David Hilliard speak to a crowd of 5,000 across the street from the Democratic National Convention.

August 17
-Communications Secretary Kathleen Cleaver, in Hawaii at the PFP convention, is refused the right to enter Japan.

August 25
-Beginning of a four-day riot in Chicago at Democratic National Convention.

-Three Panthers—Robert Lawrence, Steve Bartholomew, and Tommy Lewis—are murdered by Los Angeles police at a service station.

August 28
-Stokeley Carmichael is ousted from SNCC.

September
-The *San Francisco Examiner* prints an article exposing Panther George Murray's employment as a teacher at San Francisco State. Chancellor Dumke orders Murray's termination. The Black Student Union immediately goes on strike in support of Murray.

September 5
-The final arguments by the district attorney in Huey Newton's trial end. Attorney Charles Garry says that the trial is a diabolical attempt to put an innocent man in the gas chamber.

September 8
-Newton's jury deliberates for four days and in the end come up with a compromise verdict, convicting Huey of voluntary manslaughter. He is acquitted of the assault charge, and the kidnap charges are dropped.

-J. Edgar Hoover declares the BPP the "greatest threat to the internal security of the country."

September 11
-UC Berkeley offers a series of lectures for no credit by Eldridge Cleaver. Governor Ronald Reagan and Superintendent of Education Max Rafferty refuse to pay Cleaver's salary and order the Board of Regents to overturn the university's decision. Senator John Schmitz (a John Birch Society spokesman) sponsors a bill to withhold next year's university budget if Cleaver is not fired at once. The students respond by a sit-in at the administration building.

September 28
-Huey P. Newton is sentenced to 2 to 15 years in state prison and removed from Oakland in five minutes. Judge Friedman refuses all meetings for granting a mistrial.

-Four hours after Huey's conviction, two (admittedly drunk) on-duty Oakland police officers commit a drive-by shooting of the BPP office on Grove Street.

-Eldridge Cleaver's parole is revoked and he is sent back to prison.

September 29
-San Francisco Police officer Michael O'Brien kills Otis Baskett. Officer O'Brien is noted for wearing a "Gas Huey" button.

October
-Denver police shoot up Panther office during racial disturbance. Panther Lauren Watson is charged with conspiracy to commit arson.

-New York police department harasses Panthers over use of a bullhorn at Panther headquarters.

October 9
-Eldridge Cleaver gives first lecture on the UC Berkeley campus. On the steps of Sproul Hall he leads some 5,000 students in a chorus of "Fuck Ronald Reagan!"

October 15
-Panther Welton Armstead is murdered in Seattle.

-A warrant is issued for the arrest of Eldridge Cleaver because of his failure to appear at a hearing on the April 6 incident. Cleaver is speaking at a campus in Cambridge, Massachusetts. Charles Garry explains to the court that he had forgotten to tell Eldridge about this particular court date.

October 26
-Panthers have a fund-raising concert at the Fillmore Auditorium.

November 6
-San Francisco State college begins major strike.

November 7
-Seattle Panther Sidney Miller is murdered.

November 13
-Panther Reginald Forte's car is stopped by Berkeley police. After an altercation, Forte and Officer Wolke are wounded.

November 19
-Bill Brent and seven Panthers are arrested in San Francisco after a service station holdup and exchange of gunfire with police.

November 24
-Eldridge Cleaver disappears 3 days before he is scheduled to turn himself in to serve the remainder of a 13-year sentence for a 1958 rape conviction. He later turns up in Cuba and settles in Algeria.

November 25
-FBI memo details plans to cause dissension between Los Angeles Panthers and United Slaves (US) under the leadership of Ron Karenga.

December 1
-Forty-three Denver police raid Panther

office, cause $9,000 in damage, and steal $150 in cash.

-Bobby Seale, David Hilliard, and other Panthers attend the Hemispheric Conference to end the war in Vietnam.

December 4
-More than 500 members of the community go to San Francisco State campus to support strikers. Confrontation between strikers and police results in a number of arrests, including that of Dr. Carlton Goodlett.

December 5
-Jersey City Panthers charged with a November machine-gunning of a police precinct.

December 7
-Newark Panther office is bombed by local police.

December 12
-Twelve Chicago Panthers are arrested on weapons charges.

December 18
-Indianapolis Panther office is raided by FBI and local police, who fire three cans of tear gas and ransack the place; $600 in cash is taken from the Party's treasury.

December 21
-Denver police raid Panther office looking for weapons, but none is found. Out of frustration officers burn food and clothing that were to be given to community poor for the holidays.

December 23
-A demonstration is held by the Indiana Committee to Defend the BPP in front of the local police station. Clergy members, Citizens' Defense League, Purdue Peace League, and other community organizations are in attendance.

December 27
-Des Moines Panther office is raided by 100 police officers and FBI agents. Mrs. Joeanna Cheatom, president of the Des Moines Welfare Rights Organization, is arrested along with several Panthers.

December 28
-San Francisco Panther office is raided by police.

-Sacramento Panthers exchange gunfire in a 6-hour shoot-out with police; 13 officers are wounded and 37 persons are jailed.

December 30
-Los Angeles Panther Frank Diggs is shot in the head and killed by police agents.

1969

January
-The Panthers Free Breakfast for Children Program (FBCP) is under way at St. Augustine's Church in Oakland.

-In Chicago, Panthers Bobby Rush and Nathaniel Junior are arrested for unlawful use of weapons.

January 6

-Panther George Murray is arrested for illegal use of a bullhorn on San Francisco State campus.

January 17

-Los Angeles captain Bunchy Carter and Deputy Minister John Huggins are murdered in Campbell Hall on the University of California, Los Angeles campus, by US members.

-Panthers' national headquarters on Shattuck Avenue in Berkeley is heavily watched by local police.

January 19

-In San Francisco, the Pirkle Jones-Ruth Baruch photo exhibit on the BPP opens at the DeYoung Museum. City Hall tries to bar the exhibit.

-In Berkeley, Panthers hold a press conference announcing they do not advocate roving gangs of "bandits robbing service stations and taverns." They conclude by stating that any member who violates the rules of the BPP is subject to expulsion.

January 24

-Panther George Murray is stopped by highway patrol and arrested on gun charge.

-Chicago police and FBI conspire to prevent Panther Fred Hampton from appearing on a local television talk show.

-Funeral services for Alprentice "Bunchy" Carter at Trinity Baptist Church in Los Angeles.

January 30

-J. Edgar Hoover approves mailing of anonymous letter to provoke Blackstone Rangers to attack BPP members in Chicago.

-In Des Moines, more than 100 police officers storm the BPP office.

-In Berkeley, Judge Lionel Wilson rules the arrest of Bobby Seale illegal. The eavesdropping evidence of Officer Coyne is inconsistent with evidence.

-In Richmond, California, black police officers complain about racism and organize.

February 2

-A *Wall Street Journal* article detailing Ron Karenga's involvement with the FBI is reprinted in *The Black Panther*.

February 13

-In Berkeley 37 student strikers are arrested in the UC Berkeley Third World Strike.

February 14

-More than 600 black police officers and firemen rally in San Francisco to complain about racism and the lack of responses to their demands.

February 16

-A fundraising birthday benefit for Huey Newton takes place at the Berkeley Community Theater. Le Ballet Afro-Haiti performs along with other groups and speakers.

February 17

-John Huggins and Alprentice "Bunchy" Carter were murdered by US members at UCLA.

February 18

-Berkeley activist Tom Hayden gives speech to raise money for Eldridge Cleaver/Huey Newton Defense Fund.

February 21

-AFL-CIO approves organization of police union.

February 25

-Police attack a prointegration group at San Francisco school board meeting.

March 3

-In Chicago, Dick Gregory loses appeal to the U. S. Supreme Court challenging his conviction in a Chicago street sit-in demonstration. Gregory was one of 300 demonstrators who sat down at an intersection. Gregory is sentenced to 5 months in jail and fined $1,400.

March 13

-Attorney Charles Garry addresses members of the ACLU, speaking on "Black Justice Being Equivalent to No Justice."

-The U. S. Government promises $7.6 million in grants and loans to help private investors develop park and recreation facilities, businesses, and educational facilities in Watts. The funds for this proposed "model community" never materialize.

March 14

-In Los Angeles following a student strike meeting at Victory Baptist Church, an altercation ensues in the parking lot between US members and Panthers. Panther Ronald Freeman is wounded in the chest and groin. Local police watch the fight from their vehicles parked across the street and do not intervene.

March 17

-Vallejo, California, BPP starts FBCP with 35 children. Within a week the number of children grows to 110.

-Vallejo Party expels 24 members.

March 19

-In Eugene, Oregon, a standoff between Panthers and local police officers for alleged fire alarm tampering at the University of Oregon campus ends peacefully due to the Panthers' lawyer's negotiating tactics.

-Panthers Bobby Seale and Masai Hewitt tour Scandinavian countries: Denmark, Norway, Sweden and Finland.

March 21

-San Francisco activist Tom Hayden is arrested at federal building during a press conference against an indictment stemming from the 1968 Democratic National Convention that also includes Bobby Seale.

March 24

-Bobby Seale and Masai Hewitt return to the United States. Seale is indicted and

charged with planning the riots that occurred at the Democratic National Convention in Chicago.

-In Los Angeles, inflammatory letters instigated by the FBI are sent to Panthers from US members.

March 26

-In Des Moines, Iowa, a house used as the BPP office is completely demolished by CDT plastic explosives. Later, in testimony before the House Committee on Un-American Activities, Panthers and the local police department accuse each other of the bombing.

March 28

-In San Francisco, police officers tear gas, fire upon, using automatic weapons, and raid Party office. A total of 16 Panthers are arrested.

April 1

-In Chicago the FBCP began with 83 children, and by the end of the week more than 1,100 children are fed.

-In New York, 21 Panthers are arrested on a wide variety of conspiracy charges.

April 6

-In Oakland, a memorial for Bobby Hutton at Defermery Park, renamed Bobby Hutton Memorial Park, takes place.

April 10

-In New York, high school students hold a demonstration at Long Island City High School to demand freedom for the Panther 21 arrested on conspiracy charges.

-Students at Carver Junior High School in Los Angeles demand an end to police occupation on school grounds and inside the building.

April 11

-Confused police officers in Seattle vamp a BPP office on a phony complaint of loud noise. The entourage of 8 police cars, a paddy wagon, and tow trucks leave in frustration.

April 13

-In Des Moines, Iowa, the Panthers' FBCP is attacked by police.

-Chicago FBI initiate an elaborate scheme to arrest Panthers on illicit gun charge.

April 26

-In Des Moines, Iowa, the BPP office is totally destroyed by a firebomb.

April 27

-Thirteen members of the New York Party are purged, with their names appearing in *The Black Panther*.

-*The Black Panther* reports on the success of the FBCP. Thousands of children are fed throughout the Bay Area.

April 28

-The San Francisco BPP office is raided by local police.

April 29

-Los Angeles Panthers begin their FBCP in honor of John Huggins.

-In Chicago the FBI and local police entrap four Panthers in gun sale.

May 1
-The La Raza 7 are accused of killing a San Francisco officer. They are defended by attorney Charles Garry.

-More than 1,000 people participate in a mass "Free Huey" rally at San Francisco Federal Court.

May 4
-New Jersey BPP chapter expels 19 members.

-"Free Huey" rallies are held in 20 major cities at U. S. federal district courts.

May 13
-In Chicago an off-duty officer shoots and kills Manuel Ramos, a member of the Young Lords.

-New Jersey Panthers David Williams and Marion Fields are harassed by officers for passing out leaflets.

May 15
-A riot takes place in Berkeley at People's Park. Over 200 citizens and 70 officers are injured during the rock, brick, and bottle battle. By 6:00P.M. Governor Ronald Reagan calls in the National Guard and declares martial law.

May 17
-In Beverly Hills, friends of Panthers sponsor a day-long political awareness conference with workshops.

May 20
-In Greensboro, North Carolina, the National Guard, with tanks and helicopters, shoots up the campus with tear gas during student unrest.

May 21
-In New Haven, Connecticut, Panther Alex Rackley is viciously tortured and murdered by Panthers who suspect him of being an agent. Panther George Sams eventually pleads guilty to a second-degree murder charge.

May 22
-New Haven, Connecticut, Panther office is raided by police, and Panthers are arrested on conspiracy to commit murder.

May 23
-San Diego Panther John Savage is murdered by US members.

May 26
-In Chicago, Fred Hampton is one of 16 Party members indicted on grand jury charges ranging from stealing ice cream and distributing it to neighborhood children to unlawful use of weapons.

May 31
-In Berkeley the FBI curtails distribution of Party newspapers by ripping them up and disrupting U. S. mail service. United Airlines and TWA accept contracts to receive and deliver the newspaper, but now deny receiving the newspaper.

June 4
-In Detroit local police storm the BPP office in search of suspects in the New Haven murder of Alex Rackley; $25,000 damage is done to the office and bail is set at $4,000 each. Charges on all Panthers arrested are dropped.

-The Harlem branch purges 3 members.

-At Houston University, Bobby Seale speaks before a standing-room-only audience.

-The Liberation School, a BPP survival program, starts.

June 5
-Indianapolis, Indiana, Panther Fred Crawford is arrested for assault and battery.

-Los Angeles, Panther Daniel Lynem is charged with murder. Charges are eventually dropped.

-In Denver, Colorado, Rory Hithe and Landon Williams are arrested with no bail and charged with conspiracy in connection with the New York 21 and Connecticut 8 as well as unlawful flight to avoid prosecution.

June 6
-In Salt Lake City, Lonnie McLucas is tracked down and arrested in connection with the New Haven murder.

June 7
-The Chicago BPP office is raided in search of Panther George Sams. Eight Panthers are arrested and charged with harboring a fugitive. Bail is set at $1,000, but all charges are dropped.

-In Berkeley, a motion picture, Z, about political assassinations, has a one-day showing.

-Seventeen Panthers in Indianapolis, Indiana, are arrested and charged with disorderly conduct.

June 8
-Los Angeles Panther Wayne Pharr is charged with murder. Charges are later dropped.

June 10
-In Chicago, 16 Panthers, including William O'Neal, are indicted for conspiracy, kidnapping, and aggravated battery. Bail is set at $100,000 each.

June 13
-Panthers Joel Brown and Ron Davis are attacked, maced, and arrested by police for allegedly blocking a public walkway while selling BPP newspapers.

June 15
-J. Edgar Hoover declares ". . . the Black Panther Party without question represents the greatest threat to the internal security of the country."

-The San Diego and Sacramento BPP offices are raided.

-A free health clinic, a BPP survival program located in Berkeley, begins.

-In Oakland, a Safeway store is boycotted for refusal to donate needed food to the FBCP.

June 17
-In Chicago a number of Panthers are arrested on possession of narcotics. Bail is set at $1,000 each.

June 19
-In Chicago, Panther David Smith is arrested for selling the BPP newspaper.

June 21
-Panther William Brent hijacks a plane to Cuba.

June 23
-In Los Angeles, Elmer "Geromino" Pratt and Roger Lewis are arrested on suspicion of murder.

June 26
-Stokeley Carmichael resigns from the BPP.

-In Jersey City, 4 Panthers are arrested for carrying concealed weapons. Bail is set at $350 each.

June 28
-Eleven New York Panthers are arrested and charged with obstructed vision because there were too many people in one car. Seven are released on $1,000 bail; the remaining 4 are held for selling BPP newspapers.

June 30
-In Los Angeles, Ron Freeman is arrested on suspicion of murder and possession of drugs. Charges are later dropped.

-In Jersey City local police departments reports on the BPP before a Senate Sub-Committee in Washington D.C.

July
-In Peekskill, New York, the police attempt to burn down BPP office.

-In Jersey City, Panther Floyd Tyler is arrested and charged with murder, but soon released.

July 2
-In San Francisco, Panther Liberation School opens.

July 3
-In Chicago, Bobby Rush is stopped in a car and arrested for driving without a license plate and sticker despite the fact that the receipt is taped to the car window.

July 4
-In Oakland, Woman Power sponsors a "Solidarity With All Oppressed People" family-style picnic at Bobby Hutton Memorial Park. Speakers include Mrs. Charles Garry.

July 7
-In Washington, D.C., Ethiopian students peacefully demonstrating at the Ethiopian

Embassy are attacked by heavily armed police and tear-gassed.

July 8
-In Los Angeles, Panther Willie Calvin is arrested for selling papers and for disorderly conduct.

July 10
-In Berkeley, the PFP requests that Berkeley officer Ralph Wenly be charged with murder of a 16-year-old youth suspected of armed robbery. The PFP also calls for the arrest of Berkeley mayor, vice mayor, and chief of police as accomplices.

July 13
-In Albany, New York, 4 Panthers are stopped in car by Hudson police for no registration and two bad tires.

-San Diego police provoke a 2-day riot, leaving 2 dead, several wounded, and 100 arrested. Two officers are killed as well.

July 17
-New Haven, Connecticut, Panthers initiate lead poisoning testing. This state has the worst lead poisoning in the country.

July 18
-In Oakland, the United Front Against Fascism conference runs 3 days. The goal is to plan and discuss community control of police.

July 20
-In Queens, New York, Liberation School opens with 90 children.

July 22
-In Jersey City, a lawsuit is filed by attorneys for the American Civil Liberties Union and Law Center for Constitutional Rights to end continued harassment of the BPP by the Jersey City police department.

July 24
-The IRS targets the BPP by creating an activist organization project, Special Service Staff.

-In Baltimore, a Panther is harassed and arrested by police for carrying a machete strapped to his belt. He is found not guilty and released.

-In San Francisco, another Liberation School is started at Hunters Point.

July 26
-In San Diego, the John Savage Memorial FBCP moves ahead despite vandals who broke into the church and destroyed food.

-In Algeria, Eldridge Cleaver is cheered as he addresses the people in front of the new Afro-American Information Center. Cleaver is joined by Emory Douglas, David Hilliard, Masia Hewitt, Baby Dee, and the daughter of Richard Wright to attend a 12-day Pan-African Cultural Festival.

July 28
-In North Richmond, Liberation School opens at a recreation center.

July 31
-In Chicago, the BPP office is raided in an unprovoked attack that lasts 45 minutes. Police destroy food and take $500 in cash. Panther Pete Hayman is charged with attempted murder and is severely beaten and hospitalized.

August 1
-In Milwaukee, Panther Richard Smith is arrested for jaywalking and selling BPP newspapers.

-New York, Panthers Robert Moore and Eula May Fischer are both arrested for selling BPP newspapers without a permit.

August 2
-In Hunter's Point, San Francisco, 68 officers are armed for overkill, including a grenade launcher and Thompson submachine guns, in search of 4 men who allegedly robbed a liquor store. Doors are kicked in, sending citizens running into the streets.

-In Richmond, California, police raid the BPP office.

-In Kansas City, the BPP opens the Bobby Hutton Free Health Clinic.

-In Vallejo, the BPP issues a press release outlining community demands for 25 mph and 35 mph speed signs, stoplights, fire hydrants, and recreation park upgrade.

August 4
-In Denver, the BPP starts a FBCP.

August 6
-In Denver, a "Free Political Prisoners" rally at the city and county building is held for Landon Williams and Rory Hithe.

August 7
-Richmond officers surround BPP office in an unprovoked raid.

August 9
-In Oakland, Charles Bursey is convicted on 2 counts of attempted murder and assault stemming from the April 6, 1968 shoot-out.

-In Los Angeles, George and Larry Steiner, along with Donald Hawkins, start trial for the murder of Alprentice "Bunchy" Carter and John Huggins.

August 13
-In West Oakland the community has its first meeting at Campbell Village with Panthers to discuss community control of police petition and share grievances.

August 15
-San Diego Panther Sylvester Bell is shot and killed by US members. The FBCP in San Diego is closed due to shootings.

-In Chicago, Fred Hampton is released from Menard Penitentiary.

August 16
-Kansas City, Indiana, Staten Island, and Philadelphia BPP chapters expel members.

-In Ann Arbor, Michigan, White Panther

Party minister of information John Sinclair is convicted for selling 2 joints to an undercover officer.

August 19
-Bobby Seale is kidnapped by Berkeley police after leaving the wedding of Masia Hewitt and Shirley Neely. He is immediately taken to San Francisco and charged with initiating the riots at the 1968 Democratic National Convention in Chicago and the New Haven murder of Alex Rackley.

August 20
-San Francisco federal officers release Bobby Seale on $25,000 bond and then immediately rearrest him and secretly transport him to Chicago.

August 22
-Harlem Panthers initiate a FBCP and Free Clothing Program at All Saints Catholic Church.

August 30
-*The Black Panther* brings attention to South African political prisoner Nelson Mandela.

August 31
-In Chicago, 5 carloads of police surround Panthers near BPP office. No weapons are found, but they are accused of smoking marijuana and arrested. Later that night, officers attack the BPP office, and community citizens throw bottles and rocks at police.

September
-San Francisco La Raza opens a FBCP.
-San Francisco off-duty officer Michael O'Brien murders George Basket for allegedly scraping his car. The San Francisco police department tries unsuccessfully to cover up the murder.

September 2
-San Diego police fire bullets and gas rockets into Panther home for 45 minutes. People in the community throw bottles and rocks at police. Officers in turn kick down citizens' doors and beat the people.

September 4
-In Chicago, a federal judge orders Bobby Seale gagged and shackled to a metal folding chair and eventually removes him from the courtroom.

-The BPP in Chicago opens a free medical health clinic.

September 6
-An Algiers press release from Eldridge Cleaver condemns the action of "Mussolini" Alioto, who was traveling throughout the United States denouncing the BPP.

-The *Berkeley Tribe* newspaper reveals a transcript of a 35-step assault plan by Berkeley police to engage in a full-scale attack on the BPP national headquarters.

September 8
-In Watts, armed police terrorize children on a raid of the FBCP. Five Panthers are arrest-

ed, and again charges are dropped.

September 11
-In San Diego, Panthers Gloria Green, Plez Bolden, Deborah DeRowen, and Gloria Bolten are arrested on armed robbery charges. Their case is later dismissed.

September 12
-In Los Angeles, Panther Nathaniel Clark is murdered.

-In San Diego, Panther Gloria Shields is arrested for selling BPP newspaper.

September 15
-San Francisco, La Raza students shut down Safeway stores in support of Cesar Chavez.

September 17
-In Oakland, David Hilliard goes to court on charges stemming from April 6 shoot-out.

September 20
-Ten San Diego Panthers are arrested on suspicion of armed robbery; the charges are later dropped.

September 24
-In Philadelphia, the BPP office is raided. The FBI take file records and petitions for community control of the police.

September 26
-In Los Angeles, 6 Panthers are arrested for suspicion of burglary and stolen goods. The charges are later dropped.

October
-In New York, the Young Lords are organized by Cha Cha Jiminez.

-In Philadelphia, Barbara Coz initiates Panther Free Clothing Program.

-Advertisement for Elaine Brown's album *Seize the Time* appears in BPP newspaper.

October 4
-Chicago BPP office is raided and 7 Panthers are charged with attempted murder. Bail ranges from $10,000 to $20,000 each.

-In White Plains, New York, Bernard Clark is arrested for having an unlawful table in front of BPP office. He is found guilty and fined $25.

October 16
-Panther William Cook is picked up by White Plains, New York, officers, taken to the station, and instructed not to sell BPP newspapers.

October 18
-Panther Walter "Toute" Pope is murdered by Los Angeles metro squad in broad daylight as he drops BPP newspapers off at store.

November
-In Seattle, the BPP opens a free medical clinic.

November 7
-In Paris, France, Emory and Judi Douglas and Don Cox are harassed by customs officials and threatened with arrests. All of their

materials, such as photographs, are confiscated, and Judi is strip-searched.

November 8
-The California Conference of Black Lawyers convenes to address the Hon. Augustus Hawkins (House of Representatives) regarding the denial of constitutional rights and treatment of Bobby Seale.

November 11
-In New Haven, Connecticut, Panthers Claude Artist and Elise are harassed and beaten by police for putting up FBCP posters.

November 12
-In Los Angeles, a community meeting is in progress to finalize plans for the Bunchy Carter Free Health Clinic when 75 police raid the BPP office. The doctors, nurses and other community leaders present shocked the officers, who retreat.

November 13
-In Frankfurt, West Germany, demonstrators paint on a the wall "Free Bobby Seale."

November 15
-BPP newspaper article warns schoolchildren about drugs sold on playgrounds.

November 22
-In New Haven, Connecticut, 5,000 demonstrators march and converge at state courthouse in support of BPP members charged with murder of Alex Rackley.

November 25
-In Chicago, 13 Panthers are held in "preventive detention" on $100,000 bail for trumped-up conspiracy charges to blow up various locations.

-Emory Douglas designs 10 all-purpose revolutionary greeting cards for the Party.

-Philadelphia Panthers hold a 3-day session at the YMCA to bring together rival youth gangs.

November 28
-Bobby Seale is beaten and subjected to inhumane treatment while in custody.

December 2
-In Baltimore, Maryland, 3 boxes of BPP newspapers are lost.

December 4
-In Chicago, Fred Hampton and Mark Clark are viciously murdered by police while they sleep.

December 8
-Los Angeles police department launches a full-scale attack on Southern California Panthers in a predawn raid. At 2 separate locations, 400 officers arrest Party members and children. During one shoot-out, Roland Freeman's body is riddled with bullets, but he survives.

December 10
-In Los Angeles, Friends of Panthers, a coalition of community groups, holds a mass protest rally at City Hall to denounce the

invasion of police officers into the black community.

-Los Angeles Local Union 535, Social Services Workers' Union, passes a resolution to protest the political murders of Panthers across the country and to demand the release of all political prisoners.

December 22
-San Francisco radio announcer Roland Young is fired by station KSAN for his support of David Hilliard's speech.

December 25
-Boston, Massachusetts, Panthers receive only 2 of 7 BPP newspapers boxes.

December 26
-The entire shipment of BPP newspapers shipped to New Haven, Connecticut never arrives.

December 27
-In Los Angeles, the Bunchy Carter Free Health Clinic opens.

December 30
-Winston-Salem, North Carolina, shipment of BPP newspapers arrives a week late.

1970

January
-In Jersey City, Panthers Isaia Rowley, Charles Hicks, and Victor Perez, framed on charges of machine gunning a police station, have been locked in Hudson jail in solitary confinement for more than a year without a trial. Bail is set at $85,000 each, but due to political pressure, no bondsman will take the bail.

January 4
-Chicago Panthers open free health clinic in honor of Spurgeon "Jake" Winers.

January 6
-In Berkeley, Panthers organize community home discussion groups to talk about the Party's 10-point program, community control of police, Panthers murdered, and voter registration.

January 7
-In Detroit, Michigan, several boxes of BPP newspapers are lost.

January 9
-Panther Lee Berry, one of the Panther 21, is severely beaten in a Chicago jail and has an epileptic seizure. After emergency surgery, he is listed in critical condition.

January 17
-A federal grand jury probe threatens the staff of the BPP newspapers with possible indictments under a federal conspiracy law under the Smith "thought control" Act. All members take the 5th Amendment.

January 19
-Philadelphia police attempt to destroy the BPP office by firing into it at midnight and pouring gasoline in the doorway and igniting it. Panthers put out the fire.

January 21

-In both Atlanta and Chicago, BPP newspapers are lost, arrive late, and some are ripped.

-New Haven, Connecticut, Panther Frances Carter is told after 8 months in jail that she will be released on bail and given immunity if she testifies against the other Panthers; she refuses.

January 24
-Milwaukee's BPP chapter disbands.

February
-A San Francisco fire at the Panthers' warehouse destroys all the old issues of the Party's newspapers in stock.

-Montreal, Canada, BPP posters and newspapers are confiscated by customs officials.

February 6
-In Berkeley, the BPP Legal Defense Fund Raising Benefit features Santana, Southern Comfort, Fourth Way, and Elaine Brown at the Berkeley community theater.

-In Cleveland, Mississippi, the entire shipment of BPP newspapers is lost.

February 8
-Seattle mayor Uhlman denies a request from the Alcohol, Tobacco and Firearms Division of the U. S. Treasury Department for Seattle to participate in a raid of the BPP office.

February 15
-Huey Newton Birthday Benefits held in Berkeley, New York City, New Haven, and Seattle.

February 28
-In Brooklyn, New York, BPP newspapers arrive soaked.

March 10
-In Algeria, 6 Panthers are expelled from the international section.

March 14
-Panthers sponsor Free Food Rally at Hunters Point, San Francisco.

March 24
-In Rockford, Illinois, Panthers open 5 new sites for FBCP. They also receive request for a free medical clinic.

-Los Angeles Panther Roger "Blue" Lewis receives 10 years in prison on trumped-up charges stemming from the Panther roundup following the murders of Bunchy Carter and John Huggins.

March 27
-Milwaukee, Cleveland, and Baltimore Panthers all receive BPP newspapers late.

April 4
-In New Haven, Connecticut, David Hilliard and Emory Douglas are jailed for contempt of court and receive a 6-month sentence. Their bail is denied.

April 8
-Chicago Panthers Bobby Rush and Ed Billy "Che" Brooks refute rumors reported on television that a rift existed between them.

April 10
-Harlem Panthers do not receive their shipment of BPP newspapers.

April 12
-In New York, the Panther 21 defense office is burned, destroying legal papers.

April 17
-Oakland Panther Randy Williams and 3 other Panthers are arrested on assault with intent to commit murder and deadly weapon charge. Williams is severely beaten while in custody.

April 18
-In Frankfurt, West Germany, the Solidarity Committees of France, Britain, Denmark, Netherlands, West Germany, and Sweden meet and are informed of the illegal jailing of more than 300 Panthers; the assassination of 30 members; FBI and local police conspiracies to railroad the New York 21, Connecticut 8, Chicago 18; and excessive bail.

April 30
-Baltimore police raid Panthers' FBCP.

May 1
-In New Haven, more than 25,000 people gather in support of Panthers Lonnie McLucas, Bobby Seale, and Erica Huggins.

May 7
-Harlem Jewish Defense League pickets in front of the BPP office.

May 8
-In Chicago, the attempted-murder charges against the 7 survivors of the raid in which Fred Hampton and Mark Clark were killed are dropped.

May 9
-*The Black Panther* lists 42 BPP offices and community centers throughout the country.

-New York Panther Lee Barry, of the New York 21, is released from prison.

May 11
-FBI memo to San Francisco office directs agents to disrupt and disseminate false and divisive information to the BPP national headquarters.

May 15
-The FBI directs all agents to disrupt distribution of the BPP newspaper.

-In Carbondale, Illinois, a Panther home is firebombed, severely injuring 3 members.

May 16
-Black Student Revolutionary Conference is hosted at Yale University.

May 19
-At Kent State University in Ohio, the National Guardsmen kill 4 unarmed white students. California governor Ronald Reagan calls it "justifiable homicide."

-Detroit and Philadelphia Panthers expel several members.

May 29
-The California Court of Appeals reverses Huey Newton's manslaughter conviction. However, the court refuses to grant him bail pending the prosecution's appeal.

May 31
-Panthers in Boston open a free health clinic.

June 1
-Attorney Charles Garry files a motion for bail in San Luis Obispo for Huey Newton.
-The BPP newspaper reports on substandard housing and slumlords in major cities.

June 15
-Jaw of Raymond Lewis, editor of the BPP newspaper, is broken after he is assaulted by San Francisco police.

June 19
-In the Fillmore district of San Francisco, the BPP hold People's Community Free Festival.

-BPP expels members in Cleveland; Winston Salem, North Carolina; and Seattle.

July 3
-In Jersey City, a slumlord tries to evict a tenant for placing 2 Panther posters in her window.

July 4
-Washington, D.C. officers ransack Panther office, stealing cash and destroying office equipment and food for FBCP.

-In Cleveland, 100 police carry out a military assault against BPP office.

July 5
-Racists in Boston attack BPP free health clinic trailer by shooting at it 13 times.

July 11
-Washington, D.C. Panthers establish a free busing program to visit inmates.

July 13
-In Indianapolis, black citizens call upon the Panthers for protection from white vigilantes riding through the community on motorcycles and shooting at homes.

July 14
-J. Edgar Hoover makes the statement ". . . the Black Panther Party is the greatest threat to the national security in the history of this nation."

July 15
-In Soledad Prison a hunger strike among maximum-security inmates takes place; they demand conditions fit for human beings.

July 22
-Panthers in Berkeley and Oakland file more than 15,000 signatures to put community control of police on the ballot in the November election.

July 27
-Los Angeles police storm the BPP office.

July 31
-New Bedford, Mass., police raid Party office and arrest 21 members on charges of conspiracy to commit anarchy, inciting to

riot, and unlawful assembly. Bail totals $2,350,000.

August 1
-San Quentin inmates demand an end to forced slave labor in prison industries.

August 3
-In Philadelphia, police team tactical squads and FBI go on a search-and-destroy mission to 3 Party information centers. Officers steal money, destroy clothes, and force Panthers to strip naked; 15 members are arrested, with initial bail set at $100,000 each. Later bail is reduced to $1,500.

August 5
-More than 10,000 show up at Temple University in Philadelphia for the Party's Revolutionary People's Plenary Session despite recent raids on Party offices and pressure by chief of police Rizzo upon university staff.

August 5
-Huey Newton is set free on bail.

August 7
-In a Marin County Courthouse in San Rafael, California, Jonathan Jackson, James McClain, William Christmas, and Ruchell McGee take Judge Harold Haley, a prosecutor, and 3 jurors hostage. All three gunmen except Ruchell McGee are killed along with the judge by police.

August 8
-Chicago Panther Babatunde is found dead on railroad tracks. Earlier, police threatened to kill him.

August 11
-Several Los Angeles Panthers are given 60 days in jail for selling the Party's newspaper.

August 12
-Five Jersey City Panthers are arrested for singing a revolutionary song.

August 15
-Huey Newton gives eulogy at the funeral service of Jonathan Jackson in Oakland.

August 19
-In San Francisco, a national demonstration and mass rally to free all political prisoners takes place.

August 27
-Philadelphia officers raid Panthers' Information Center.

September
-In Washington, D.C., The People's Revolutionary Constitutional Convention takes place.

September 15
-Two hundred New Orleans police officers raid Panthers' office.

-Toledo, Ohio, officers riddle Panther office with bullets, wounding Troy Montgomery. Montgomery is forced to lie in the street for 2 hours.

September 26
-Los Angeles Panthers sponsor a youth conference.

October 3

-A Panther delegation, including Elaine Brown and Eldridge and Kathleen Cleaver, visits North Korea; North Vietnam; and Peking, China.

October 11
-In Oakland, a "Free Bobby Seale" benefit takes place at the Sportsman Club.

October 13
-Angela Davis is captured by law enforcement agencies.

October 16
-The Jamaican BPP branch is destroyed by fire.

-Julio Rolden, a Young Lords' Party leader, is found murdered in his cell.

October 19
-Conspiracy charges against Bobby Seale are dropped.

-In Detroit, 600 police officers with 2 tanks and automatic weapons raid Panther office; 15 Panthers are arrested. The community responds by throwing rocks and bottles and burning 4 police cars.

November 1
-The Lumpen, the BPP's musical group, makes first appearance at People's Free Benefit.

November 13
-In Algeria, the international section of the BPP hosts visitors from South Africa's ANC and ambassadors from China, North Korea, and Ethiopia.

November 25
-New Orleans police launch attack on Party office.

November 30
-The city of Oakland plans to close Merritt College. The campus lease expires March 31, 1971.

December 4
-The masses in Chicago come out to pay tribute to assassinated Panthers Fred Hampton and Mark Clark.

1971

January 23
-Huey Newton expels Los Angeles Panthers Elmer "Geronimo" and Sandra Pratt.

February
-Huey Newton and Eldridge Cleaver disagree on San Francisco talk show. Newton expels Cleaver and the entire wing of the international BPP

March 5
-Eldridge Cleaver expels Huey Newton and David Hilliard from the BPP.

August 21
-Panther George Jackson is assassinated in San Quentin Prison.

December 15
-Huey Newton is freed after third mistrial from officer John Frey charges.

December 31
-H. Rap Brown's anti-dope movement is

launched in New York.

1972

March 29
-Huey Newton alters the BPP 10-Point Program.

June
-In Los Angeles, Elmer "Geronimo" Pratt is convicted of murder and sentenced to life in prison.

1973

April
-Elaine Brown runs for Oakland City Council, and Bobby Seale runs for mayor of Oakland.

October
-Oakland's BPP Youth Institute moves into a larger building, renamed the Oakland Community Learning Center.

1974

Summer
-Huey Newton is charged with pistol-whipping a tailor and killing a teenage woman.

August
-Huey Newton and girlfriend Gwen flee to Cuba. Elaine Brown becomes Party leader.

1975

November 18
-Eldridge and Kathleen Cleaver return to the United States from Paris.

December
-The BPP files a $100 million lawsuit against the FBI.

?1976/7?

January
-The Senate Intelligence Committee discloses the FBI report documenting its work to neutralize the Party.

1977

July 3
-Huey Newton returns to the United States from Cuba.

1980

January 3
-Eldridge Cleaver is freed on 5 years' probation after pleading guilty to assaulting officers in the April 1968 shoot-out.

June 15
-Huey Newton receives a Ph.D. degree in the history of consciousness at University of California at Santa Cruz.

1982

-The last BPP survival program, the Youth Institute, closes its doors due to lack of funds.

1988

-Historian Runoko Rashidi films BPP member amongst the untouchables in Australia, England, Japan, Palestine, and India.

1989

August 22
-Huey Newton is killed in West Oakland.

SOURCES

By Ula Y. Taylor & J. Tarika Lewis

All of the quotations and material from the historical sections of this book are documented in the following texts.

Earl Anthony, *Spitting in the Wind,* Santa Monica: Round Table, 1990. This is a confessional text from a former FBI agent.

Elaine Brown, *A Taste of Power: A Black Woman's Story,* New York: Doubleday, 1992. This memoir gives much information on a black woman coming of age during the sexual revolution, the latter years of the Black Panther Party.

Stokeley Carmichael and Charles V. Hamilton, *Black Power: The Politics of Liberation in America,* New York: Vintage Books, 1967. This book is one of the first attempts to deal with the multiple meaning of Black Power.

Clayborne Carson, *In Struggle: SNCC and the Black Awakening of the 1960s,* Cambridge, MA: Harvard University Press, 1981. The best historical treatment of the Student Non-Violent Coordinating Committee.

Ward Churchill and Jim Vander Wall, *Agents of Repression: The FBI's Secret War Against the Black Panther Party and the American Indian Movement,* Boston: South End Press, 1990. The best book providing overwhelming evidence about the FBI's campaign to neutralize the Black Panther Party.

Eldridge Cleaver, *Soul on Ice,* New York: Dell, 1968. Collection of prison letters and autobiographical writings that has become a classic.

Adam Fairclough, *To Redeem the Soul of America: The Southern Christian Leadership Conference and Martin Luther King Jr.,* Georgia: University of Georgia Press, 1987. One of the best historical works on the Southern Christian Leadership Conference.

David Hilliard, *This Side of Glory: The Autobiography of David Hilliard and the Story of the Black Panther Party,* Boston: Little Brown and Co., 1993. This classic memoir is important because the author documents his activities with comments by other Black Panther Party members.

Gerald Horne. *Black and Red: W. E. DuBois and the Afro-American Response to the Cold War 1944-1963* (NY: State Univ. Press, 1986). This text details the lack of activism by leading civil rights groups during the Cold War.

George Jackson, *Soledad Brother: The Prison Letters of George Jackson,* New York: Bantam Books, 1970. George Jackson letters unveil his extraordinary courage, insightful analysis of American society, and reasons why he became a beloved freedom fighter.

Edward Keating, *Free Huey,* New York: Dell, 1970. This book, written by one of Huey Newton's attorneys, offers a blow-by-blow discussion of his manslaughter trial.

Reginald Major, *A Panther Is a Black Cat,* New York: William Morrow, 1971. One of the first texts published on the Black Panther Party by an eyewitness and scholar. It is a must read for anyone interested in the Party.

Gene Marine, *The Black Panthers: The Compelling Study of The Angry Young Revolutionaries Who Have Shaken A Black Fist At White America,* New York: Signet Books, 1969. This is one of the earliest books on Black Panthers written by a Ramparts editor.

August Meier, Elliot Rudnick & John Bricey (ed) *Black Protest in the Sixties: Articles from The New York Times* (NY: Markus Wiener Pub., Inc. 1991). This text is a compilation of the cutting edge articles in The New York Times.

Huey P. Newton, *Revolutionary Suicide,* New York: Ballantine Books, 1973. This autobiography gives much detail on the founding of the Black Panther Party and Huey Newton's life after prison.

Huey P. Newton, *War Against the Panthers: A Study of Repression in America,* University of California, Santa Cruz, June 1980.

Kenneth O'Reilly, *Racial Matters: The FBI's Secret File on Black America, 1960-1972,* New York: The Free Press, 1989. This book includes one chapter on the Black Panther Party detailing the ferocity of FBI officials.

George Otis, *Eldridge Cleaver: Ice and Fire!,* Van Nuys, CA.: Bible Voice, 1977. This book documents Eldridge Cleaver's Christian conversion after he returned from exile.

William L. Patterson. *The Man Who Cried Genocide* (International Pub. 1971). Attorney Patterson and Paul Robeson discuss their petitions to the United Nations charging the United States government with genocide against black people.

Hugh Pearson, *The Shadow of the Panther: Huey Newton and the Price of Black Power in America,* Reading, MA: Addison-Wesley, 1994. The accuracy of this book on the Black Panther Party and African American history in general is questioned by some scholars.

Bobby Seale, *A Lonely Rage: The Autobiography of Bobby Seale,* New York: Bantam Books, 1978. Offers undisclosed personal details about Bobby Seale and the evolution of the Black Panther Party.

Bobby Seale, *Seize The Time: The Story of the Black Panther Party and Huey P. Newton,* Baltimore, MD.: Black Classic Press, 1991. The most important book on the early history of Black Panther Party.

Malcolm X, *The Autobiography of Malcolm X,* New York: Grove Press, 1966. This classic memoir continues to have a profound impact on African Americans.

Committee on Internal Security House of Representatives, *Gun-Barrel Politics: The Black Panther Party, 1966-1971,* House Report No. 92-470. This report details why the federal government perceived the Black Panther Party to be a threat to United States security.

Committee on Internal Security House of Representatives, *The Black Panther Party, It's Origin and Development as Reflected in it's Official Weekly Newspaper, The Black Panther Community News Service,* House Report No. 91, October 6, 1970.

The Black Panther Party, *Supplement to the Whole Earth Catalog,* The Evolution Quarterly, Fall 1974.

Roy Wikins and Remsey Clark, Search and Destroy: A Report By the commission of Inquiry into the Black Panthers and the Police, New York: Metropolitan Applied Research Inc., 1973.

The following newspapers were consulted for the historical section of the book. *The Black Panther Community Newservice.* (the Black Panther Party newspaper is the most important primary document on the weekly activities of the organization), *Berkeley Barb, The Flatlands, Oakland Tribune, San Francisco Chronicle*

PERMISSIONS

2-3: Jonathan Eubanks
4-5: AP/Wide World
10-20: AP/Wide World
22-bottom: Jonathan Eubanks
25: Samuel Brooks
27: Jonathan Eubanks
28: The Black Panther "Newspaper"
29-top: Jonathan Eubanks
30: AP/Wide World
31-32: The Black Panther "Newspaper"
33-top: AP/Wide World
33-bottom: Samuel Brooks
34-39: AP/Wide World
40: Samuel Brooks
42: AP/Wide World
43-44: Ron Riesterer/Oakland Tribune
45: AP/Wide World
46: The Black Panther "Newspaper"
48-49: Emory Douglas
50-51-top: Matilaba (J. Tarika Lewis)
51-bottom: Emory Douglas
52: Jonathan Eubanks
54: Roz Payne
56: The Black Panther "Newspaper"
59: Ron Riesterer/Oakland Tribune
60: AP/Wide World
61: Jonathan Eubanks
62-right: The Black Panther "Newspaper"
62-left: The Bettmann Archives
63-64: Jonathan Eubanks
65: Roz Payne
66: Jonathan Eubanks
67: The Bettmann Archives
68-69: AP/Wide World
70: Black Panther Party
71-top: AP/Wide World
71-bottom: The Bettmann Archives
72: Roz Payne
73-76: AP/Wide World
77: Black Panther "Newspaper"
78: AP/Wide World

79: Samuel Brooks
80-top: The Bettmann Archives
80-bottom: Samuel Brooks
81: The Black Panther "Newspaper"
83: Howard Bingham
84: AP/Wide World
85-top: Ron Riesterer/Oakland Tribune
85-bottom: Jonathan Eubanks
86: The Black Panther "Newspaper"
87: AP/Wide World
88-top: Ron Riesterer/Oakland Tribune
88-bottom: Library of Congress
89: Library of Congress
90-91: AP/Wide World
92: Roz Payne
94-102: AP/Wide World
103-105: Jonathan Eubanks
106: AP/Wide World
107: The Bettmann Archives
109: Samuel Brooks
110-111: AP/Wide World
112-top: The Bettmann Archives
112-bottom: AP/Wide World
113: Roz Payne
114-top: The Bettmann Archives
114-bottom-116: AP/Wide World
117: Jonathan Eubanks
118: AP/Wide World
119: Samuel Brooks
121-122: AP/Wide World
123: Samuel Brooks
124: The Black Panther "Newspaper"
125-128: AP/Wide World
129: Robert Zuckerman/Gramercy Pictures
130: Shelley R. Bonus/Gramercy Pictures
132-157: Robert Zuckerman/Gramercy Pictures
158-top, right: AP/Wide World
159-top: Robert Zuckerman/Gramercy Pictures
159-bottom: The Black Panther "Newspaper"
162-163: Robert Zuckerman/Gramercy Pictures
164-top, right: AP/Wide World
166: Robert Zuckerman/Gramercy Pictures
170-171: Robert Zuckerman/Gramercy Pictures
172: Shelley R. Bonus/Gramercy Pictures
173: J. Tarika Lewis
174: Courtesy of David Hilliard
175: Robert Zuckerman/Gramercy Pictures

POLYGRAM FILMED ENTERTAINMENT PRESENTS
A WORKING TITLE PRODUCTION
IN ASSOCIATION WITH TRIBECA PRODUCTIONS
AND MVP FILMS
A MARIO VAN PEEBLES FILM

Kadeem Hardison as Judge
Bokeem Woodbine as Tyrone
Joe Don Baker as Brimmer
Courtney B. Vance as Bobby Seale
Tyrin Turner as Cy
Marcus Chong as Huey Newton
Anthony Griffith as Eldridge Cleaver
Nefertiti as Alma
James Russo as Rodgers
M. Emmet Walsh as Dorsett

Casting by Robi Reed-Humes C.S.A.
Music Supervisor Larry Robinson
Original Music by Stanley Clarke
Costume Designer Paul Simmons
Film Editor Earl Watson A.C.E.
Production Design Richard Hoover
Director of Photography Edward Pei
Executive Producers Tim Bevan • Eric Fellner
Screenplay by Melvin Van Peebles based on his novel "Panther"
Produced by Preston L. Holmes, Mario Van Peebles and Melvin Van Peebles
Directed by Mario Van Peebles

A Gramercy Pictures release, U.S. and Canada
Polygram Filmed Entertainment International, all other countries

INDEX

ABOUT THE AUTHORS

Mario Van Peebles, director and co-producer of Panther, is a versatile and talented actor, director, and most recently, author. His feature film directing debut, in the critically acclaimed New Jack City, as well as his breakthrough multi-cultural western, Posse, have established him as one of the most distinguished young film directors in the country. Van Peebles received a Director's Guild Nomination for Malcolm Takes a Shot, a CBS movie. For acting, he has been awarded a NAACP Image Award for his work in Heartbreak Ridge opposite Clint Eastwood and a Bronze Halo Award for his performance in the CBS movie, Children of the Night.
He received a degree in economics from Columbia University and was recently awarded a Doctor of Humane Letters degree from Hofstra University.

Ula Y. Taylor, Ph.D., the chief historian in the Department of African-American Studies at the University of California at Berkeley, has earned such honors as a fellowship with the Schomburg Center for Research in Black Culture (to pursue her work on the history of Amy Jacques Garvey), the Ford Foundation Minority Dissertation fellowship, and the University of California Presidential fellowship. For the producers of Panther, Dr. Taylor contributed a historical annotation of the shooting script. A native of Pasadena, California, she now resides in Oakland.

J. Tarika Lewis, alias Matilaba, the first female member of the Black Panther Party, served as an on-the-set consultant to the film during production, and is noted for her illustrations in the Black Panther Community Newspaper. Now a graphic designer and musician (she often performs with jazz artist John Handy), she has been working on her chronology of events relating to the Black Panther movement for several years. She lives in Oakland, California.